D0394768

RUNNING for JESUS

Photo by Sandy La Corte

Madeline Manning Jackson

RUNNING for JESUS

as told to Jerry B. Jenkins

WORD BOOKS, Publisher
Waco, Texas

ISBN 0-87680-460-1
Library of Congress catalog card number: 76-56483
Printed in the United States of America

To my mother, Queen Saulsberry, for all her prayers;
my coach, Alex Ferenczy, for all his time and
confidence; and
my son, Little John, for his love and potential

M.M.J.

And to Gary Lee Shiffman, a brother in Christ

J.B.J.

CONTENTS

PREFACE

Evelyn was drunk. She was black, just past middle-age, well dressed, and pretending to be wealthy. Lugging her red suitcase and staggering through the Cleveland airport, she drew disgusted stares. Evelyn fell into step with Madeline and me as we exited toward the parking lot.

"What route you takin', honey?" she asked Madeline, as if she knew her.

"East Cleveland," Madeline said. "Can I drop you somewhere?"

"I need to get to Ohio," Evelyn slurred.

Madeline took her suitcase. "You're *in* Ohio, dear," she said.

"I mean Ohio *Street!*" Evelyn said, stopping and jamming her hands on her hips. "Is that out of your way?"

It was, and it was late. But Madeline didn't say so. "I can take you there," she said. "Come on."

"I'll pay you *any*thing," Evelyn said, nearly in tears. "*Honey*," she whined, drawing out the first syllable, as she would do during the entire trip, "you name it. I'll pay you *any*thing."

Madeline introduced me as the writer from Chicago

9

who had come to write a book about her. We had just met
and had hardly had a chance to get acquainted. In Madeline's car, Evelyn monopolized the conversation for more
than an hour, jabbering incoherently about various business transactions that had fallen through that day, and
how her friends had left the airport without realizing that
she had missed her plane.

Madeline followed her directions to a gas station, where
Evelyn ordered the attendant to buy her two packs of
cigarettes and a can of orange pop from the vending machines. Then we were off to a house she was trying to sell.
Then to a rundown residential area. After more than twenty
miles and three stops, Evelyn was home.

"Now, *honey*," she said, "how much can I give you? I'll
pay you *any*thing."

"I don't want any money," Madeline said.

"What? Oh, you are the sweetest thing. Here, let me
give you something."

"No. I don't want your money. There is something you
can do for me, though, Evelyn."

"*Any*thing, *honey*."

"You can let me pray with you."

"Oh, I'd like that. Would you? I'd *love* that. You're so
sweet. I go to church and I'm a Christian and I'd love for
you to pray with me. You wanna pray with me, really?"

Madeline ignored her nervous ramblings and took
Evelyn's hand in hers. I watched from the back seat as
Madeline began, "Lord, thank you that you brought us
together tonight in your wisdom. . . . I pray that Evelyn
will know that you love her and that you want her to be
strong and to live for you and to resist temptation and to
give herself completely to you—"

Evelyn began to shake her head from side to side. She
whimpered and pulled her hand away, raising her arms.
Madeline kept praying. "No, no, I can't take any more,"
Evelyn cried.

Madeline continued, "Be near to her in a special way—"

Evelyn buried her head in her hands. When Madeline finished, Evelyn was sobbing. "You don't think I'm a Christian!" she said.

"God knows your heart," Madeline said.

"I'm a Christian!"

Madeline let her cry. When Evelyn calmed down, she was no more articulate, but she gushed with thanks. "God will help me because you cared for me," she said. "You are so sweet. You're a lovely child."

"Praise the Lord, Evelyn."

"I do, *honey*. I do. And thank you too, Larry." She reached a hand back to me.

"Jerry," I corrected.

"Of course, Gary," she said. "You two will keep praying for me, won't you?"

We both nodded and Evelyn trudged off into the night.

My first impression of Madeline Manning Jackson.

JERRY B. JENKINS
Wheaton, Illinois

Chapter One

To the STORE *and* BACK

To understand me, you'll need a bit of an understanding of what it means to run a half mile as fast as you can. Don't go out and try it!

What enters your mind when you hear the words *a half mile?* If you can't relate to the distance at all, clock it on the odometer of your car or bike. Then walk it sometime. It should take you about ten or eleven minutes. Maybe it's just down to the store and back.

For me it's twice around a quarter-mile oval. Eight hundred and eighty yards. You've seen the shape and dimensions on television if you've ever watched a track meet, and many college football stadiums have tracks surrounding them too. Running on one looks fun, doesn't it? It can be, but it's not easy.

Since I hold the American records for women in both the half mile (or the 880, as it is generally called) and the 800-meter (the metric equivalent, which is a few yards short of a half mile and is run internationally and at the Olympics), the kind of company I usually run with can cover the distance in less than two minutes. That isn't fun. It's torture.

But the rewards! It can actually be exhilarating. For some reason, the pain of running a winning time of two minutes and five seconds is much easier to take than the agony of running a second-place time of 2:05.

What goes into running a world-class half mile? First, of course, training. I don't know of any women runners at that level who appear to have an ounce of fat on their bodies. They are finely tuned running machines and have spent hours sacrificing and working to eliminate all the barriers to running a good race. My coach has always told me that strategy means nothing if you're not in shape.

The reason is simple. Say you've planned to hang back a few strides behind the leader until the last 60 yards or so. Then you want to make your move. If you're not in decent shape, you'll never stay that close to the leaders for that long. And if you're not in top shape, you may stay with them that long but have nothing left to call upon for your big strategic finish.

But what about when you're in top shape and you hang with the leaders all the way and have strength left to pass them and sprint to the finish, but—

But they're in top shape too. You make your move and they make theirs. Then what? What separates the women from the girls? There are many names for it. Crude ones like *guts*. Polite ones like *determination, drive, stamina*. Some attribute it to background. Was it an advantage for me to be a black girl from the ghettos of Cleveland when all the other women running the 800 at the 1968 Olympics were white, Asian, or European? Perhaps.

Maybe I had more to think about during that crucial last lap. When it was just the top eight 800 runners left in the world, all in top shape, all with guts and determination, all with speed and endurance. We were moving, chugging around, no one giving an inch or expecting one. What made it possible for me to break away from the pack?

I wasn't consciously thinking about my background. I

was confident in my ability because I had been well coached and trained hard. Maybe subconsciously I *was* reaching back to the instincts that helped my brothers and sisters and me survive street life. When it came down to the last 60 meters, I would not be denied.

There are other things you must understand to really get to know Madeline Manning Jackson. I hope you'll find them in the following pages. There's a spiritual side of me which goes beyond my athletic ability. Sure my bit of fame has come through my running, but track was never really what I was *all* about. What I'm really all about is Jesus. I hope that will be obvious. He used my running career to give me a platform from which to tell others about him. Most of my story is about all the places I've been and the races I've run and some of the people I've met. But most of all, I want what Jesus has done through it all to come through clearly.

It's great to look back and think about having run in three Olympic games by the time I was twenty-eight years old. And there are incidents surrounding each Olympiad that I think you'll find exciting and dramatic and even shocking. But rejoice with me as I remember the people who have come to Christ during the running career that sent me to the Games.

If you're interested in music, my story is for you too. Don't get me wrong. If you are neither musically inclined nor familiar with track and field, I still think there's a lot here for you. So much of my story is just personal. I'm like anybody else. I have gone through some pretty rugged times, and I have spent years searching for myself and for my place in this crazy world. I think you'll be able to identify with me even if you have never won a medal or cut a record.

There will be a few terms you might not understand, but most will be self-explanatory. For instance, a *kick* is the last sprint in a long race to the finish. It's that last surge where you abandon all thoughts of your lack of air or strength and just run as fast as you can.

If I talk about the *stick,* I'm probably referring to the baton, a hollow tube that relay runners carry and hand off to each other. *Oxygen debt* is a physical state in which you have demanded too much of your system too soon (by running too far too fast) and there is not enough oxygen in your blood to keep up with the needs of your body.

When I talk about running a *leg* on the relay team, I mean one of the four segments. And if someone in track talks about *running a 56* or *breaking two,* he means running a quarter of a mile or 400 meters in 56 seconds or running a half mile in less than two minutes.

Enough on that. Most of those inside terms are insignificant compared to the experiences I relate, but if one has you puzzled and it slipped by without my explaining it, write to me. My address is at the end of the book, but don't look now. You can write to me about anything. I'd love to hear what you think of my story. I've even had people send me advice, though most of my mail is from people who want prayer. I *do* answer my mail.

So, what turns a skinny little ghetto child into an Olympic gold medalist? How does she deal with a broken home, spinal meningitis, her own divorce, raising a son alone while working and training for the Olympics? And what happens when God calls her out of retirement a second time, just to run for Jesus?

You'll know soon.

Chapter Two

The CEDAR AVENUE PROJECTS

The identification tag on my bed was not in sight that January day in 1948 when Cecil Manning peered through the glass for a first look at his newborn daughter. But he didn't have any trouble identifying me. "Mine's the one with the long feet," he told the nurse. "That one there with those big, long feet kickin' away."

She checked, and he was right. He just knew, he told me years later, that the daughter of an athlete would have athletic-looking feet. I've still got 'em.

As a toddler I idolized my father to the point where I held my index finger in the same position he did. His had been deformed by a break years before. Mine was an imitation, but it flattered him. "That's my daughter," he'd say, smiling. "The one who holds her finger like mine."

My mother, Queen, had two other children at home by a previous marriage, but I was Cecil Manning's first daughter. Having been a baseball player, he wanted an athlete. Before I was even old enough to know what that meant, I almost ruined it for him by contracting spinal meningitis.

I was only three years old, but for three months I was deathly ill, and for a month I was so delirious I didn't

17

even know my parents. For six months my back was sensitive and I lived in fear of getting more shots. Mother prayed for me constantly, even after the doctors had become pessimistic, and she reminded me often in later years that it was the faithfulness of God that brought me through.

Some of my earliest memories are of my mother praying. It made me curious, this strange habit of bowing before the Lord. Sunday school and church intrigued me too, but it was Mother's praying that really made an impact on me. She would sit me down with Myrtle and Robert and pray with us every day.

Myrtle and Robert. Myrt was a beautiful girl. She was enough older that she mothered me a lot when I was a child. She and Robert fought over me because I was the baby, a weakling because of my illness. I used to pretend to be asleep whenever we arrived home, so someone would have to carry me up the stairs to our apartment.

Home was in the Cedar Avenue Projects in the metro area of downtown Cleveland. It was a ghetto filled with blacks, poor whites, and other minorities. And it drove my father to drink. Even as a youngster I knew something was terribly wrong when Mom would yell at him for coming home drunk in front of us kids. He was basically a quiet, gentle man, and he never attacked her or anything. A couple of times he yanked the phone off the wall or threw something, but then he would go sleep it off. It seemed he was sleepy drunk most of the time.

It hurt me because I also had good memories of Dad. I loved to watch him sing in the male chorus of the Mt. Hermon Baptist Church. With his beautiful hair parted down the middle, and in his best suit, he was a great looking man. But as he began to drink more and more, his once-strong faith in Christ was pushed back into the background and he gradually quit going to church. He had been a well-liked, outgoing type, but drinking made him hide in a shell.

Mom fussed and fussed until he got tired of staying around home much. When he did show up, he was drunk. Myrt and Robert and I used to search out his bottles and pour them down the drain and replace the booze with water. Oh, that made him mad, but he never spanked me. He was crazy about me, and he still is.

By the time I started kindergarten at Sterling Elementary School, I didn't see Dad often any more. I was puzzled and hurt, and I was perhaps a little more worried than the other kids were about my mother leaving me at school the first day. I hadn't been exposed to very many kids my own age, and I was hesitant. Besides, I had been having bad dreams about my dad.

More than once I ran into my parents' bedroom in the middle of the night, crying over a nightmare. It was always the same. I would be in heaven looking into hell and seeing Dad burning and screaming. I would run all over heaven trying to find Jesus to see if he could let Dad take punishment for just a little while and then let him come to heaven. "He didn't mean it," I'd plead. "He's sorry and he won't do it again!"

But Jesus would always say that it was too late, and I'd wake up crying. Mother always prayed with me for Dad, and years later our prayers would be answered.

Occasionally I had good dreams too. They were always about my going to heaven on a ladder or up some stairs, and angels were all around. Those dreams were beautiful. The combination of dreams, Mom's prayer life, and what I heard and saw at church and Sunday school made me incredibly inquisitive, and from the age of five on I asked my mother questions about Jesus every day.

I was the one kid Mother didn't have to badger to be ready on time. I was always ready for church. Even when I wasn't entirely sure what all was going on in the 1,000-member congregation, I enjoyed hearing Pastor Fuller preach.

Dr. Robert L. Fuller could really get excited about the things of God. Of course these were emotional services, and I wouldn't have missed them for anything. Most of all I liked the fact that Dr. Fuller had become a Christian at a very young age. In fact, he was a child prodigy. He had been *the* pastor of a church in the South when he was just five years old. That's right. Of course, older men ran the business end of things, but he was the one who ministered from the Word. He had had a speech impediment until he tried to preach; then the Holy Spirit would take over and he would preach with the anointing of God.

He occasionally spoke about his childhood experiences, and they were my favorite stories, along with those of David and Goliath and Daniel in the lions' den. One Sunday when Dr. Fuller was recounting how he had been used of God even as a child, he began to cry. I was moved. I was only eight years old, but I knew I wanted God to use me in some way too.

There were still things I would have to learn about God. I discovered that he was a God of love, not of condemnation. And that he loved me enough to die for me and rise again for me. I leaned over to my mother. "Mom," I said, "next Sunday I want to accept Jesus."

"What?" I think she wondered, *Why next week?* I told her again. I simply wanted a week to think about it, to see if it was for real—to prepare myself for it somehow.

All during the week I prayed that God would forgive my sins. The week became more intense with every day. On Sunday I was the first one dressed and ready for church. We left early and got there before the doors opened. I didn't even hear the sermon. When the invitation was given, I tell you, I was ready. I was so small and skinny, with long legs and long thick hair in pigtails, they had to stand me on a chair so Pastor Fuller could see me. He asked me if I believed in Jesus and if I knew that Christ had died for my sins. Despite the huge crowd, I was so ready that there was no shyness. I answered each question loud and clear, and the congregation echoed their assent with each exchange. I received Christ into my life that day.

I learned my first valuable spiritual lesson soon after that when Mother came down with pneumonia. Going into her sickroom one evening, I asked, "Mom, would you let me pray with you?"

"Sure, honey."

I knelt beside her bed and yelled at God. "Hey, Jesus!" I said. "Uh, my mom's sick here, so would you mind healin' her? She said you're a doctor. Amen."

The next morning I charged into her room, pigtails flying, expecting her to be up. "How you feelin'?" I asked, scaring her half to death.

"Oh, not too well today, Madeline," she said, weakly.

"Well, why not?" I demanded.

"I feel a little worse than I did yesterday with a fever and all. I think the doctor is going to put me in the hospital for a few days."

I was nearly in tears. "But I *prayed* for you!"

"Madeline, not always does the Lord answer right in your time, you know. You have to sometimes wait upon the Lord."

I didn't know what that meant. All I knew was that I had prayed and God hadn't answered. If waiting on the Lord meant praying some more, I was willing. I fell to my knees again, and in my eight-year-old innocence and honesty, chastised God. "Hey, Jesus," I said, "I told you yesterday, you know, that my mother is sick here. I wanted you to heal her. Now what's wrong? You too busy up there or something? I want you to heal her."

Mom tried to tell me what it meant to wait upon the Lord, but she was too weak and I wouldn't have understood anyway. What I did understand, however, was that when the doctor arrived that afternoon, he announced

21

that her fever had broken and that she was going to be all right.

"I frankly don't understand it, Mrs. Manning," he said.

Mom chuckled. "Well, my daughter just told the Lord to get back on the job, and he did."

That was my first lesson in faith, and I never forgot it, especially when I was being chased by gangs, or getting beat up at school.

Mother bought me little Bible story books to read, and they made everything very vivid for me. Another thing about Mother's influence on my faith was that she always did what she could to provide a peaceful environment for us to grow up in, even in the middle of the ghetto. The families downstairs would have shouting matches and drunken brawls and even knife fights that would scare me and give me nightmares, but Mother always kept her own household under control.

She hassled my father for his drinking until he was gone more than he was home, and then she was strict with us to the point that she would not allow us to fight and holler and carry on. I'm so glad I didn't have to experience first-hand the kind of fights that went on downstairs. Whenever I would find myself in the wrong place at the wrong time and see the feuding families take after each other down there, I ran upstairs and hid, crying. I hated fights. Even the thought of someone actually knifing someone else—I couldn't stand it.

In spite of all the problems with Dad, I wasn't really ready for the news that he and Mom were going to split up permanently. I'll never forget leaving the courtroom with her and her asking who I wanted to live with. "Me or him?"

I couldn't say anything for a while. Finally I broke down. "Both of you," I sobbed. "I want both of you. Why can't you stay together?" I realized later, of course, that she couldn't have stayed with him, but it was too much for a child to grasp, and I think Mom regretted having asked the question.

We moved to a slightly bigger apartment (there was more money in the house because none of it was being thrown away on booze). But Mom had to do housecleaning, and the job of looking after me during the day fell to Myrt and Robert. After school and all day during the summer, they were responsible for protecting me in the ghetto. It was no easy job. There is no minimum age limit for gang members or their victims in the Cedar Avenue Projects.

I had transferred to Marion Elementary for first grade and was really learning the consequences of not joining a gang. Non-gang members were fair game. We were chased, taunted, beaten up, and generally threatened. If it weren't for my first love, I might never have survived elementary school in the projects.

Jerome Calloway was a street-wise nine-year-old, and if you think I'm exaggerating about gangs at this age, you're wrong. I was afraid of Jerome because he was a gang leader, and he was always sending one of his honchos to drag me to him. The only boy in the school who could catch me was Grasshopper, a six-foot elementary school student, believe it or not. And even he couldn't catch me if I got much of a head start. The ghetto had taught me to move fast.

I was usually able to get out of facing Jerome, and unlike other girls, I was not about to fall head over heels for him and treat him like a big shot just because he was a gang leader. I was afraid of him, but I didn't respect him, and most of all I wanted nothing to do with him. Interestingly enough, that's what attracted him to me.

Once after school I broke one of my mother's rules by inviting some cousins in while Mother was not there. And who should waltz in right behind them but Jerome? I'd like to have died. "You've all got to leave," I said. "I just remembered my mom told me I couldn't have anybody in." I shooed them out, but Jerome stayed. Now what was I going to do? Worse yet, what was *he* going to do?

Chapter Three

THANK GOD for LITTLE WHITE BOYS

To my surprise, Jerome was terribly gentlemanly and asked if he could sit down. "Well, really I'm not supposed to have company, and my mother will be here any minute—" It was a lie.

"I just want to talk with you," he said. "Every time I try to see you, you run the other way. You must think I'm really bad."

I lied again. "It's not that I think you're bad or that I'm afraid of you, Jerome. It's my mother. She—she doesn't want me hanging around all those gang people."

"Well, I can take care of that," he said. "I like you as a person and I don't want to see you get hurt. Let me protect you so you don't have to run from gangs any more. If everyone knows you're my girl, you won't have to run any more."

That sounded like a pretty good bargain to me. I was so impressed by how nice and straightforward he was that I fell for him instantly. It meant no commitment on my part. I just let him walk me home and hang around with me outside at school, and I was protected.

During the summer, Jerome wasn't around, so poor Robert

had to watch over me. He was really athletic, and he wanted to run everywhere. I was skinny and frail and still anemic from my illness, so it was hard for me to keep up with him at first. He had to hold my hand when he ran anywhere, and he'd spend most of his day dragging me around the projects full speed, complaining all the way. Even now he claims he made me the runner that I am today!

Though he resented it, he made the best of it. After making me run around the neighborhood with him—my legs almost falling off in the process!—he'd brag that no girl could outrun his sister. Other boys would say, "All right, bring her on!" But I beat every one of their sisters. And after I beat them running, they'd want to fight. I hated that.

"I don't want to fight," I'd tell Robert. And usually he'd get me out of it. But once he didn't. After I outran a girl, she started pushing me. I cried. "I don't want to fight, Robert." The girl's brother and several other kids gathered around.

"She's pushing you, Madeline," Robert said. "You'd better not let her pick on you. If she hits you, you hit her back." The girl took it as her cue and slapped me. That was it. I went wild. I was trying to put her in her grave, I was so mad.

After I beat her up she threatened to go get her knife. "Let's go, Robert," I said, crying.

"Oh, she ain't gonna get no knife. She's just talking," Robert said.

Even her brother told her, "You might as well quit. This girl done outran you and turned around and beat you. You might as well just hush. You bring a knife out here, she's likely to make you eat it."

He was right.

All the while, this running and romping was building my little body to the point where it was hard to tell that I had been sick. I wasn't really supposed to have been doing such strenuous things, and maybe that's why I did them. I didn't want to be the weakest, the smallest, the underdog. I loved stories about children who overcame barriers. I loved the story of David killing Goliath, and, while Daniel was not a child, I was thrilled with the story of just one man like him in a den of ferocious lions. I would not be defeated or put down. I would excel, I would defend myself.

Mother didn't appreciate my being such a tomboy, especially when she had been instructed by the doctor to keep me from too much activity. By the next year in school I was anxious to compete against boys. There wasn't a girl around who could even come close to me in a foot race. The white boys thought it was great sport to tease me and taunt me until I got mad enough to chase them.

"I bet you can't outrun *me*, nigger," they'd shout while I sat there fuming. They thought it was the funniest thing in the world when I would start crying. Usually I would just take it because I was still basically easygoing. I really hated confrontations. But I had my limit.

When they pushed me too far, called me too many names, or convinced me they really didn't think I could either catch them or beat them up, I would light out after them, crying and shouting. Once I started after them, I wouldn't stop until they were caught. I jumped over fences, swung through trees, and climbed over garages. And I always caught them. By the time I caught them, I was so mad I'd punch two or three of them at a time. Maybe that's what gives me so much fight today. It may not have been the Christian thing to do, but I could not understand why I should endure such abuse. If they were gonna dish it out, they were gonna have to take it too. If it gave me the drive that has made me a champion, then thank God for the little white boys.

One game I really loved was called bullrush. Someone was selected to start in the middle and everyone else would line up at one end. We would all run past the person in the middle and try to make it to the other end without getting tackled. Whoever got tackled joined the one in the middle and the rest of us would run past them the other way and try to make it to that end.

With every run past the people in the middle, more and more kids would get tackled. The one person left running at the end would be named queen of bullrush. But if the queen ran past everyone without getting caught, he or she became king. It was rare, because by the time there was only one person left running back and forth, there were at least fifteen in the middle trying to tackle him.

One day I was determined to be king even if it killed me. I made it easily during the first several passes to the other end, relying on my speed and getting lost in the rush. When there were just a few of us runners left, I tried varying my strategy, running fast, then slow, then dodging, sneaking around someone. Soon I was the only runner left. I had to get to the other end to be queen, then back again to be king. There were more than fifteen kids in the middle, waiting to nail me.

On my first solo run to the other end I went full speed and dodged tacklers at the last instant to make it. But now they were on to my strategy. As I took a few minutes getting back my wind, I rocked back and forth, getting ready to speed through the crowd again. I decided I would change my strategy one more time and run at the weakest person. When he tried to tackle me, I would push him into the next person, try to spin off and turn on the speed.

The crowd in the center was restless. They taunted me to come on. I took a deep breath, rocked back and took off. They converged on my path, but I dodged some of the boys and drove toward the smallest tackler. He tried to trip me up, but I shoved him back into the next guy, pivoted and raced toward the sideline, arms and legs flailing. I made it! For a week after that, everywhere I went it was "Hail to the king." In a way it was my first "athletic" victory. I loved it. I hated to lose.

Playing bullrush and jumping over fences were the two most fun things I could think of. It's a wonder I didn't become a hurdler. I had a favorite tree too. I don't know why, but I most loved to hang in that tree when Mother put this cute little dress on me. Something about hanging from a branch by my knees with that dress hanging down over my head, blowin' in the breeze—

I got the worst whippin's for that. "I'm trying to make a lady out of you," Mother would say. "Would you kindly stop tearin' up your skirts and dresses?" I still like that tree. I'm gonna have to go back one day and see if it's still there.

The only spanking I ever got in school was someone else's fault. A girl named Judy liked Jerome, so we never got along from day one. He passed me one of those "I-love-you-do-you-love-me?" notes in class one day, and she intercepted it. Was she mad!

"Just wait till I get you outside," she hissed at me. "And Jerome, don't you say nothin' to me."

The teacher Miss Huff (Tough Huff, we called her) looked up. "You'd better keep that noise down back there," she said.

Judy kept picking at me and cussing. "Oh, shut up," I said finally. Guess who Miss Huff heard talking? She made me come to the front of the room and hold my hands out while she smacked them with a ruler.

"That was Judy causing all the fuss back here," Jerome called out. I loved him for that.

"Then do you want to come up here and take the spanking for Madeline?" Miss Huff asked.

"Sure," he said.

"Then come up here. I'll give Madeline a few less whacks." So I still got some welts on my hands. I cried and cried, but the ruler hardly fazed Jerome, he was that tough.

I had never really gotten over my fear of Jerome. I always had this dread that he might try to molest me or something. That was what gang leaders were supposed to do. He never tried anything, though. I suppose he had enough other girls. He always treated me like some sort of a princess, and I loved that. He knew I was a Christian and that there were certain things I wouldn't do and didn't like, and he respected me.

My Christianity manifested itself in the neighborhood too. I enjoyed imitating Mother, and when I wasn't playing baby dolls and housewife, I was outside mothering the younger kids in the area. Whenever I saw little kids who seemed hungry, I dragged them home and fed them. I'm not sure what Mother thought about it all, but when she saw that they were really hungry, she'd say, "All right, go wash your hands."

She made the greatest black-eyed peas, and we served the kids peas and cornbread until it seemed we could have no more. But there was always enough for the next day. I think there were times when we had more after feeding a bunch of kids than we did otherwise. If that sounds like a miracle, then maybe it was. We never went hungry, and neither did anyone else in the neighborhood, if I could help it.

Maybe I mothered little kids because I missed having two parents. I don't know. I often asked Mother if I could see Dad, wherever he was. "No," she'd say, "he's in no condition—" I didn't know what she meant. Kids are all forgiving. I forgot the bad times and remembered the good. I didn't like not having a daddy, and when I found out Mom was going to marry Preston Saulsberry, a member of our church, I was overjoyed.

He was an employee of the local General Motors plant, but he was also a minister and preached at various churches. I was nine when he married Mother, and I think I was a little too much for him to handle. Robert and Myrtle were in their teens by then, but a nine-year-old, active, talkative, gregarious girl was a bit much for a man who had never had children. I jumped in his lap, hugged him, asked him a million questions, and generally made a nuisance of myself. I can't blame him for being a bit cold toward me, but since he didn't respond the way I thought a daddy should, we never got along well until seven or eight years later when I could talk with him more as an adult and a mature Christian.

Having another source of income did wonders for Mother and the household, of course, and now she could take me out of public school and get me some religious training. I fought it tooth and nail when she first told me she was going to have me transferred from Marion to Zion Lutheran School. But she was fed up with the gangs and the crowded classrooms. All she ever heard about were fights and hassles, and she wanted me to go to school where I would learn more about Jesus.

I was convinced that Zion Lutheran School would be like a jail: dry, no fun, no familiar faces. If I'd had any idea that Zion would mean the beginning of what was to become an international track career, I'd have jumped at the chance to go.

Chapter Four

ALEX

I had been in the fifth grade for just a few weeks at Marion School when I switched to Zion. I had just gotten to know all the kids in my class and was really enjoying myself. The fact that Marion was so noisy and crowded and understaffed didn't hit me until my first day at Zion.

I hardly knew what to make of it. Here was a nice facility with all kinds of activities, medium-sized classes, plenty of personal attention from the teachers, and a release time half an hour earlier than the public schools in order to cut down on fights.

By Christmastime I felt part of what seemed like one big, happy family. We sat in large groups to sing carols, and we took our time, going over each song carefully so several kids had a chance to try solos. That's where I first realized my potential as a singer. I had always loved to sing along in church, but I never knew how much fun singing for people could be until I tried it at Zion.

Through the end of fifth grade and all of the sixth, I became popular with the rest of the kids because of my singing. I had always figured I'd never be popular because I was so skinny and (to me) ugly. I enjoyed being appreciated and being somebody, but I never let it go to my head. The popularity I received from singing solos was nothing like the glory I'd receive from being a champion in track and field. Luckily the singing and running success came in stages, so I was able to learn to cope with it. I always knew down deep that in spite of my excelling in either music or track, I was just like everyone else. I never let anyone get to know me without my getting to know them too. I've never wavered from that. I don't want anyone to ever be able to say that I became too big or too important to take time for others.

The man who introduced me to track was Phil Wambsganss. He came to Zion as a new teacher in the fall of 1960 when I was beginning seventh grade. Mr. Wambsganss was enthusiastic and had all kinds of ideas about how Zion should have a track team and should be competing in the statewide Lutheran elementary school competition.

I loved to run and jump and play, but the only thing I had ever heard about track was that Wilma Rudolph, a black woman, was the fastest woman in the world. It must have been something I heard on the news related to the 1960 Olympics, but as a twelve-year-old, I didn't even know how anyone knew she was the fastest. It inspired me to know that the fastest woman in the world was black, and I thought maybe I could be the fastest someday, but I wondered, *Did they see her running down the street and just decide she looked the fastest, or what?*

Mr. Wambsganss answered those questions. He started a program to see how fast we could run and how far and high we could jump, so we learned about taped measurements, running certain distances, and being timed by a stopwatch. What a love-hate relationship I would develop with the stopwatch in the years ahead!

Soon after I got involved with the new track and field program at Zion, Mr. Wambsganss encouraged me. "You're

an outstanding singer and an outstanding runner," he
said. "If you choose either as a career, you'll do well." The
principal, Mr. Sieboldt, encouraged me too to stick with
whatever I chose to do so I would be a success. It meant a
lot to me that he took the time to talk personally with students, and I never forgot the counsel of both those men.

I did well in the school-against-school competition in
the seventh grade, and when the statewide meet came up
at the end of the season, I was ready. I won the standing
long jump, the triple jump (a hop, step, and jump), and
both sprint races; and I was named the all-around state
athlete of the year.

I won all the same events the following year, but with
better distances and times, of course. I had become the
real heroine of the school, and it gave me a big-sister type
of feeling. Kids would look up to me and treat me as if I
were someone special. That's when I learned that I had to
be warm and friendly to everyone. That was and is the
only way to be.

The officials at the school wanted me to join the Lutheran church, but as an impulsive junior higher, that wasn't
for me. "It's too quiet around here," I'd say of their church
services. I liked my own Baptist church where things
would really hop. That isn't to say I didn't see Christ in
many of the teachers and students, but I wasn't about to
change churches. My mother couldn't afford the tuition
for the Lutheran high school anyway, so when my class-
mates were graduating from eighth grade and looking
forward to high school, it was back to the public school
system for me. Ninth grade was still junior high in the
Cleveland public schools, so I headed for Patrick Henry
Junior High for one year. Talk about a fish out of water.

Again I was in a new situation where even the few
people I knew hadn't been in school with me for three
years. It was no longer Madeline the popular, Madeline
the heroine. It was just Madeline, the new girl.

I hadn't fought since I was a little girl, and I had learned from my mother and my time at Zion to be quiet and reserved. Perhaps it wasn't entirely for the best in my case, because I still had a breaking point. I let myself get walked on or pushed around for only so long.

I had been at Patrick Henry long enough for most of the kids to know I was a nice, quiet person, and long enough for the teachers to know I was a good student, one they would never have any trouble from. But there was one girl who took a dislike to me for some reason—a light-skinned black girl from a bad family. She was short, very thin, and had red hair, and she cursed at me every time she saw me. That really offended me because my mother had taught me not to curse, and that kind of language was something you rarely heard at Zion.

After several days in a row of having her call me a "long, skinny, old ————" at every possible opportunity, I had to say something. "Why you always calling me names and picking at me? I don't even talk to you. I don't bother you at all." She didn't answer, but a few days later it all came to a boil.

The little redhead was several places behind me in the cafeteria, and I hoped she wouldn't even see me. I dreaded facing her and tried to avoid her every day. She had me frustrated to the point where I didn't know what to do. I got my food and a bottle of chocolate milk, my favorite, and had been seated for just a few minutes when she sat down at the other end of my table.

"Where's my milk?" she asked. A few other girls giggled. I think one of her friends must have taken it and hid it—as a joke. I ignored her. "Where is it?" she demanded, louder this time. I looked up. She caught my eye and saw my bottle of chocolate milk. "You took it!" she shouted and moved to my end of the table.

"This is my milk," I said evenly as she grabbed it. I hung on.

"It is not! You took it off my tray! I had it right there!"

"This is my milk," I insisted, my patience worn thin after weeks of taunting. "Just leave it alone!" With that she jerked the milk from my hand and in one motion drove her fingernail under the cap, popped it off, and splashed the whole bottle in my face.

I went wild. I grabbed the table and stood up, flipping it over. I jumped over the table and grabbed her by the collar with one hand and by her skirt with the other and threw her against a glass partition separating the tables from the kitchen. It knocked the wind from her and she was out cold. I just stood there shaking. Of course, everyone came running. The others girls stuck up for me, telling the whole story, but none of the teachers needed to be convinced anyway. Knowing both of us and seeing that milk all over me was all the evidence they needed. I was glad to find out that she wasn't seriously hurt, but I was also glad that she never hassled me again.

I wanted to run on the track team at Patrick Henry, especially after having done so well at Zion Lutheran. The competition among the public schools was much tougher, of course, and I was anxious to see how I could do. Trouble was, I didn't even hear about the track tryouts until a day after they were held. I begged for the chance to try out anyway. The coach refused.

I talked to Diane, the fastest girl on the team. "You know I can beat you," I said. "Tell the track coach."

She did. "Madeline can beat me, and if you don't believe me, we'll race."

"Just let me try," I chimed in. "If you'll just give me a chance, I'll prove it to you!"

Diane was the state champion and had run the 50-yard dash in 5.8 seconds, extremely fast for a ninth-grade girl. (That's fast for a ninth-grade boy, come to think of it.) The teacher figured if I was foolish enough to think I could beat the state champion, I might as well try it. So she let us race.

In the fifty I beat Diane by just inches. But in the 100-yard dash, I left her by about twenty yards. Do you know that coach still wouldn't let me on that team? The girls were as furious as I was. "You're just throwing away talent," they told her, but that only made her more stubborn. She had let us race only to see if I was for real. She never intended to let me be on the team whether I won or not.

I was deeply hurt. I really thought I could do something for Patrick Henry, and beating the defending state champion showed me where I stood in relation to all the other statewide public school runners. My grades weren't bad, but they weren't good enough to get me any recognition. And I wasn't part of the in crowd. Without track, I couldn't be somebody. I was just Madeline.

Until the next year, that is.

In the fall of 1963 I enrolled at John Hay High School and began the tenth grade. I was tall, awkward, and shy. Boys who had been buddies were now looking at me as more of a young lady. I just wanted to run, which I hadn't done competitively for more than a year. I was sick when I learned that I could have run in the Junior Olympics program during the summer, but by not being on Patrick Henry's track team, I had missed out on the information.

I gravitated toward the music department at John Hay, hoping to find my niche. I joined the mixed chorus and the girls' glee club and I began to become known as Madeline the singer. I loved singing, but though I didn't know it, I wasn't through with athletics yet.

In gym class I excelled in the physical education tests. My teacher, Marilyn West, saw qualities in me she thought should be developed. She encouraged me to become a gym leader, which included a wild initiation where I was sudsed up, slid through, whacked, and every-

thing else they could think of. I joined the basketball team
and the volleyball team, but Miss West's best idea was
getting me on the girls' track team.

"Would you like to run for the school?" she asked.
What a question! I'd been wanting to run again since
eighth grade. I joined the John Hay team too late in the
season to go to the state meet, but I was running again,
and that was all I cared about. I ran the 100- and 220-yard
dashes until Miss West talked me into trying the 440 (a quarter of a mile), because she had no one else who could handle the distance. I enjoyed the quarter, but I considered
it more than a sprint. At about the 330-yard mark you're
dead, and after that it's a matter of just gutting it out.

During the first part of my junior year of high school in
the fall of 1964 I really came into my own as a quarter-
miler. I became the first girl in the history of the school to
run the quarter in less than 60 seconds. It was then that
Miss West, who was also a manager of the Cleveland Department of Recreation track team (now known as the
Cleveland Track Club) told the CDR track coach about
me. Alex Ferenczy showed up at the next meet.

Since the meet was at John Adams High School, not
far from where we lived, my mother came to watch me
run for the first time. It was providential. I broke the sub-
60-second barrier again, and after the race Alex came to
me. "You run real well," he said, in heavily Hungarian-ac-
cented English. "I'd like you to run for the city team."

I didn't know what to think. In fact, I wasn't entirely
sure I had understood him correctly. Being shy, and with
the instructions of my mother not to talk to strange men
(or, should I say, men who are strangers?), I said, "Anything you've got to say to me, see Miss West and my
mother over there in the stands."

Of course Miss West had to interpret for him, but somehow they got through to Mom that he wanted me on his
team. "It's up to Madeline," she said. "Ask her. If she

wants to, it's all right with me, as long as you take care of her and get her to and from wherever she's supposed to be."

I still wasn't sure what it was all about, but I welcomed any chance for good competition. Running for the city sounded important, too. Before the 440-yard run at my next meet Alex told me that I was going to "run a fifty-seven." *Yeah, sure,* I thought. But already Alex knew me better than I did. Trackwise, anyway. I was just running. He saw all the potential, and he knew what I could do.

I looked forward to running for him and training under him, but I might not have been so eager if I had known what the first day of practice would be like.

Chapter Five

EVERYBODY but ME

To make it on time to my first workout under Alex, I had to go directly from basketball practice. I was wearing a gold shell blouse, green shorts, and long, gold knee socks. What a sight! The other girls eyed me warily, wondering what I might be able to do with those long, skinny legs. They were all worried about their positions on the team until I took off running on an indoor track for the first time.

Without experience on the tightly banked track, I could hardly maneuver the turns. My legs went flying every which way, and those girls would like to have laughed me to scorn. They'd never seen such a funny-looking crane plowing around a track, falling all over the place—and they let me know it.

Another thing the girls hassled me about was what I called Alex. I couldn't say Ferenczy, but I had been raised to be respectful, so I called him Mr. Alex.

"What you call him Mr. Alex for, girl? His name is Alex, call him Alex!"

"I can't," I said, and Alex stood up for me.

"Leave her alone," he'd say. "She's respectful and she's

disciplined, and that's the way she was raised. I wish some of that respect would rub off on some of you."

The other girls would turn away snickering, but they were worried about their places in the world. There was something about the funny-looking girl who called the coach Mr. Alex. She had an inner drive that pushed her to learn fast, and she worked hard perfecting her technique and mastering the indoor track.

I wanted to be a sprinter, but Alex said, "No way, not with those long legs. The quarter mile at least, and maybe longer distances." He tried to tell me the quarter mile was really a sprint, and it was true that I hit full stride in it. But to me it was a long way, and running it well was agony.

When the other girls stayed in their cliques and pointed at me and sniggled and made fun of me, I had to decide whether to quit the team or work harder. All I knew was that I wanted to run. There were a few Olympians on the team—Eleanor Montgomery and Vivian Brown—and other top runners like national champion Sandra Knott who ran longer distances. Alex had me run with her for endurance, and while she could run me ragged at first, I determined to stay with her no matter how much it hurt.

Round and round that track she'd run me until my legs throbbed and my lungs begged for air. When I'd think I couldn't run another lap, she'd pick up the pace and I'd push for a little more. I had more endurance before I knew it, but Sandra kept running farther faster. She made me fiercely competitive because I didn't want to admit I could not keep going. I stayed with her and stayed with her and stayed with her until even Alex was amazed. "You can't shake Madeline," he'd shout, laughing. "She's going to be good! She's got determination! She'll stick in there no matter what! You can't get rid of her!"

I'd hold my head a bit higher and demand more of my legs and lungs, trying to remember the economy of mo-

41

tion and the fluidity Alex preached. Sometimes I could tell just by the way this white man looked at me that he saw something in me that I didn't see. Alex quickly lost color in my eyes, and I learned in later years that he was working without pay, suffering with officials who made him raise traveling money and with parents who expected him to do everything for their girls. He just loved track and what it could do for people.

I was to become living proof of what a good track program could do for a person, but back then all I knew was that Alex was a hard-driving coach who took pleasure in seeing us do well. And he cared. What else mattered? I would have run my heart out for him.

By the winter of 1964 I could run with any of the girls except high jumper Eleanor Montgomery. Her legs were so long that I couldn't get around her indoors, but I outran everyone else and developed the beginnings of a running style Alex confides to others is "like a thoroughbred." (He won't say it in front of me. As long as we've been friends, and as flattered as I am that he'd compare me to a beautiful running machine like a thoroughbred, he still thinks it would be crass to liken me to a horse in front of me.)

During the Christmas break in December of 1964 we were really into high gear, training for the Amateur Athletic Union indoor national women's track and field championships in New York City in January. I beat everyone except Eleanor in the 220-yard dash workouts. And in the 440 no one could touch me. I led the way in the endurance drills too. I wasn't sure what the nationals were all about, but I knew I was ready. Everyone else had been to the nationals before and talked about the pressure and the excitement. I couldn't wait. I wanted to be more than ready. I wanted to be a team leader and to make Mr. Alex proud of me. I wanted to show my stuff and be a national champ. Could I win the 440, or help one of our relay teams win? I was sure of it, and every day in practice I felt stronger. The worse it hurt to run long and hard, the better I knew I would do in January. The girls said big crowds packed the indoor arena, and that there were all kinds of newspaper reporters and photographers and other media people there. I was going to make a name for myself. I would be somebody. I would be Madeline Manning, track star. Nationally.

Alex gave several of the girls a ride home each day after practice, and I was often the last one. More than once when we got downtown and saw the neon signs blinking everywhere, Alex would say, "Your name could be in lights some day, Madeline." I'd laugh. I thought he was crazy. I knew he was just saying it to make me work harder, but I wondered if he really thought it could happen. Regardless, it worked. I pushed myself to such levels of speed and endurance that I couldn't wait to put myself to a real test like the indoor nationals.

I didn't even know that the girls who did well at the nationals qualified for a U.S. team that traveled in Europe. I knew only that the national championship was the top meet of the indoor season and that it was a showcase of talent—a showcase I wanted to be in.

One night about two weeks before the big meet in New York, Alex took the other girls home and began to talk slowly as we headed toward my house. "Madeline, I know you are going to be upset, and you're not going to understand, but I want you to trust me." I turned quickly to face him. "I am not going to take you to the nationals in New York," he said.

I was stunned. I couldn't believe it. "Why?" I nearly shouted, on the verge of tears.

Alex kept his eyes on the road. "All right, all right, just wait a minute," he said. "Let me explain. Now Madeline, all the other girls have experience from last year, and—"

"But I beat 'em all. I worked so hard—"

"I know, but it's not your time yet. You're still young

and you've got so much to learn. I want you to go when you're ready to take everything. I know you can do it. And I'll know when you're ready. You can't just go out there and run because you're fast. You have to know what's going to happen in relays too."

I couldn't understand that to save my life. I was deeply hurt. I stared out the window as he drove on. "It's not your time," he whispered again. "Trust me, I'll know when." I needed time to let it sink in, but before I got out of the car, Alex told me he had drawn up a workout sheet for me to use while they were gone. *The audacity!* I thought. *I'm supposed to work out during my vacation from school while they're all at the nationals having fun and winning medals?*

For some reason the disappointment and even the fact that the other girls teased me about not going didn't dampen my determination. I ran harder than ever during the workouts before the nationals. No one understood why I bothered, but Alex noticed. He knew what I was made of.

After Alex and the girls left for New York, I studied the sheet he'd left with me. It called for strenuous lonely workouts on Monday, Wednesday, and Friday. No competition, no coach. It's usually hard to push yourself when you're the only one working out, but having never been out of Cleveland before, and having counted so much on going to New York, I didn't find it difficult. I told myself over and over that when that team got back, they were going to see what being in shape was all about. If I had any weaknesses, they would be gone by the time the team returned. I would run everyone off the track. As I worked out my bitterness and frustration I drove myself harder and harder, being careful not to hurt myself and following Alex's written instructions to a T.

He had really devised a strenuous regimen, and if anything, I made it more difficult. I never slacked off. I pushed and pushed and whipped myself into a finely tuned running machine. I don't know where I would have fit into the national scheme of things, but I knew one thing by the time the girls returned: I was as fast and as in shape as I could be at that stage of my life. I hadn't grown to my full height yet, and a more mature musculature would come with age, but for then, I was as fast and as good as I could be.

I couldn't wait until Alex brought the team back to practice so I could show my stuff. I wanted them to know that I would be ready for the outdoor nationals. Their first day due back came and went and the only person who showed up was Alex. I was furious. Not only did he give them a two-week vacation after they had done well at the championships,* but he also came to the track to supervise my workout! Again I thought, *the audacity of this man!*

Well, if he was the only one I could run for, I'd run for him. I did everything he asked, and I was blazing. He smiled a lot, and I think he knew what had gone on while they had been away. He too was anxious to see how the girls would react to my increased strength and speed.

When they finally returned to practice, they'd done nothing for two weeks. I had stacked workout upon workout, and I was ready. Alex had me lead a few endurance drills, and the girls hated it. I ran them to death. The sprinters would complain, "Let us work on shorter distances, we don't need this."

I'd say, "Don't complain. Come on, this is good for you. You'll be able to really tear up in the sprints if you build your strength." When I thought of what our relay team could do if everyone sacrificed to get in shape, I switched to encouraging rather than taunting. A real team spirit

---

*Eleanor had won the high jump, Sandra had placed in the 880-yard final (that told me how I might have done), and the relay teams had done well too.

developed, and even during the grueling time trials when Alex had us running against the clock, we'd yell and scream for each other. The team was growing closer, and we were all running better.

In retrospect, I'm sure the bitter disappointment of missing the indoor nationals in '65 helped make me the disciplined runner I am today. I had always worked hard, but I didn't really know what I had in me until I pushed myself to the limit out of sheer frustration. I don't know what else could have driven me to it.

In school I'd been known only for my singing up until that time. I sang in solo contests and with the mixed choir and girls' glee club, where I also led the singing occasionally. Some of the kids knew I ran too, because I would run a relay now and then with the school team before going to practice under Alex. But it wasn't until the summer of 1965, right at the end of my junior year, that I made a name for myself at school as a runner.

I had been driving myself so hard with the city team and running so infrequently at school that I was about to unleash a surprise on the city and state. In the girls' public school city finals I broke records in the 220-yard dash and the 440. And in the state finals I ran the 440 in 59 seconds in the qualifying heat, 58 seconds in the semifinal, and 57.5 in the final. No one in Ohio had come close to that, and it nearly equaled the national record for high school girls.

All my hard work for the city team under Alex had wound up paying off for the school. With another year of high school to go, I was the state champion. More important to me, though, was that the Amateur Athletic Union *outdoor* national women's track and field championships were scheduled for Columbus, Ohio, in June. Alex had me scheduled to run the 440-yard dash in the girls' division, and I was scared to death of my first national competition.

Chapter Six

ICE CREAM
All Over the CAR

I was so nervous I could hardly get myself together. Sleep was nearly impossible, and I had to force myself to eat to keep up my strength. It wasn't until after the first qualifying heat, which I won easily, that I calmed down and realized that I could do well. The emotional shebang was over. I was still nervous and excited, of course, but that dread—that fear that you're in way over your head and may make a fool of yourself—was finally gone.

In fact, relaxing a day between the qualifying heats and the semifinals helped a lot. I was even stronger for the semis, and I was able to think clearly and strategize. I was careful to run my own smooth pace and not to break away from the pack so fast that I had nothing left at the end. I tied the American record in the girls' division, winning my semifinal heat in 57 seconds flat.

Before the finals the next day, my nervousness returned. Though I was now coholder of the American record for my age group, I wondered if I had burned myself out. Could I do it again? Had the other girls saved themselves for this one and were they capable of doing even better than my record?

I was ready nonetheless. As I stood on the line, waiting for the gun to sound, I decided I could only do my best. *No one is here to fail, especially me. I'm gonna give it all I got, and may the best lady win.* I threw my head back and let my arms dangle free. On tiptoes I shook my whole body loose.

At the gun I started fast and strong. Even my pacing and coasting near the halfway point and into the last curve was smooth and swift. I led all the way. Into the last straightway I felt an exhilaration, adrenalin shooting through me and eliminating fatigue as I realized I would win. I broke the finishing tape in 56 seconds flat, putting the age-group record out of reach and becoming national champion. At seventeen, I had become the first girls' division national champion ever from Cleveland.

Alex and the rest of the team were thrilled, of course, but the real attention getter in the meet was our medley relay team. In the medley, the first girl runs 220 yards, second and third run 110 yards each, and the last runner (me in this case) runs 440 yards to finish a four-girl total of 880 yards. The other girls were older, so though I was seventeen, our relay team was entered in the women's division. Now I was sure I was in over my head. Some of the other anchorwomen had run in the *women's* division 440-yard final, and the winning time had been almost two full seconds faster than my girls' division record.

The only way I figured we could win would be if our team was already leading when I took the baton. We had been working hard, and as our times improved, we had begun to hope to make the relay finals. Now we had made it, but could we win? Few thought so.

My personal choice for the medley relay favorites were the Tennessee State Tigerbelles. They were the talk of the meet, as they had been every year, sweeping all the sprint races and leading in team totals. Of course, I had never heard of them before, but anyone who had followed women's track and field knew they were the best team in the country almost every year. They were coached by Ed Temple, they were all black, they gave track scholarships, and they were proud of their reputation. When the Tigerbelles came onto the track, everybody took notice. Wilma Rudolph and Wyomia Tyus, both Olympic champions, had come from Tennessee State, as had a dozen other world class tracksters.

But the Tigerbelles didn't really have a strong quarter-miler that year. No doubt they would be leading after the first three sprinters had run, but their anchorwoman, Estelle Baskerville, kept telling me, "Madeline, you don't have anything to worry about. You're a quarter-miler and I'm not. (She was primarily a long-jumper.) By the time I get the baton, you'll be halfway around the track." I wasn't so sure.

When the gun sounded, Gloria Woods carried the baton for us. She was in the middle of the pack somewhere at the 220-yard mark when she handed it off to Natalie Allan for the next 110. Natalie was in last place when she passed the stick to Debbie McDonald, and though she had only 110 yards to run, poor Debbie faded quickly after trying to make up the distance all at once. She had brought us back to seventh place out of eight teams, but I knew we'd lost. I was screaming for her to "come on, come on!" but California's anchorwoman, in first place, was already coming out of the far corner. I had a whole straightaway to run before that point, and I figured she'd be on the backstretch before I got the baton.

Alex was shouting from the sideline, "Madeline, you can do it! You can do it!" I winced at him and pointed to the leader. "I can't. I can't do it!" He was mad. "Just go out! Go out!"

That meant to give it all I had. No time to strategize or pace. If I wanted to catch her, I was going to have to catch her. She was the only one I had to worry about. If

I caught her, I'd have to pass five other girls in the process. *All right, Alex,* I said to myself, *I'll go out. If I don't have anything left at the end, that's just too bad.* Debbie slapped the baton into my palm and I took off.

I ran it like a 100-yard dash, as if I needed to save nothing for the finish. By the end of the straightaway I caught the sixth-place girl and burned into the curve. Moving wide, I blew past the fifth-place and fourth-place girls. As I came onto the far straightaway I was making up ground on Estelle Baskerville. At least we were going to beat Tennessee State if I had anything at all left for the finish! I passed her and found myself in third place.

Ahead of me, running for Mayor Daley's Youth Foundation Chicago team, was Norma Harris, who had finished second in the women's division 440. I could hear the track announcer calling the race: "Here comes Madeline Manning of the Cleveland Track Club in the red and black. She's moving up!" I determined not to fall apart but to try to concentrate on my form even though I was running a crazy fast pace. I had no choice. As I tried to battle past Norma at the 330-yard mark, I felt as if I might waver. I had been in an all-out sprint for over 300 yards.

Alex had run across the infield and was standing inside the curve with the Tennessee State Coach Ed Temple. Everyone was scared of him, including me, but I had already passed his runner. I could see him and Alex out of the corner of my eye. Alex was jumping and shouting, "Now move, Madeline! Now move!"

I thought I was moving already. Did he think I had anything more left? As I flew around the corner, Coach Temple, who had been standing with his arms folded across his chest, suddenly jumped up and yelled, "Go ahead, Manning!" It totally blew my cool. I couldn't believe he'd be pulling for me. My body was screaming for rest, but with Alex and Ed Temple there cheering me on, what could I do but run until there was nothing left?

I passed Norma in the middle of the curve and only the California runner remained ahead of me. She appeared steady, but I was gaining on her. The crowd was standing, shrieking. I was going to do it! The seventeen-year-old from Cleveland, out of her class in the women's division, was going to pull it off! I caught her coming off the last curve and sped into the straightaway, pulling away from her and winning by several yards. I had sprinted the entire quarter mile, and one of the stopwatches clocked me in 52.5 seconds. It was officially listed at 54, but a couple of other timers had me in under 53 as well. It was the highlight of the meet and I was high for hours. I was clapped on the back, carried around, hugged by everyone, and generally given the heroine treatment. What a night!

Good things come in bunches. Ed Temple asked me if I was interested in running at Tennessee State after high school. "Sure," I said.

"Stay healthy," he said. "And I'll send you a full scholarship." Then the AAU announced that I had been chosen to run the 440 for the U.S. team in Russia, Poland, and Germany later in the summer. Janell Smith Carson, who had won the women's division in 54.1, was the first quarter-miler, but the slowest stopwatch on my relay leg had me a full second faster than Norma Harris's time in the open quarter, so she was selected as the 440 alternate.

When Miss West brought me home from Columbus, Mom met me at the curb. "I'm going to Russia, Poland, and Germany," I said, matter-of-factly.

Mother took it just the way I'd said it, without really hearing. "Oh, that's nice," she said.

"Let me tell her," Miss West said, as I grabbed my stuff from the car. The next time I turned around, both Mom and Miss West were crying.

"Come here, baby," Mother said. "You're going overseas." It had hardly hit me yet.

My older stepbrother asked if he could take me out and

show me off to some of his friends. "Sure, Pete," I said.
"Okay." He called a cab and we went cruising around
Cleveland so he could brag on me to all his buddies.
Between stops he had the cabbie stop at a Dairy Queen
where I got an ice cream cone. As we sat there eating,
finally not saying anything, it all washed over me.

I had never been outside Ohio. In fact, the trip to
Columbus was my first trip out of Cleveland. Now here I
was with a meet scheduled in Kansas City, then three
more on the other side of the world. I screamed, "I'm
going to Russia! Russia!" Ice cream flew all over the car as
I hugged Pete.

"You mean it's just getting through?" Pete laughed.

"Germany and Poland!" I cackled. The cabbie cracked
up.

"I wondered if you were really Madeline Manning," he
said. "I thought your brother was lying all this time, but
I believe him now."

Janell and Norma and I ran in Kansas City in a final
tuneup before going overseas. The committee had voted
that Norma would still run in the international competition, though even if she finished first or second, she
would not count in the scoring because she was the alternate. Needless to say, she felt she should have been the
second quarter-miler, based on her second-place finish in
the women's national. I hoped to prove that they had
made the right choice by doing well in K.C., though our
finishes would not change anything, regardless.

For Janell, a strong, short-striding powerhouse, Kansas
City was home. Her parents, her family—everybody who
knew her was there. They had been waiting for a chance
to see her debut before the hometown crowd. Jim Ryun,
also a local hero, had just graduated from high school
there and had become an international star as a miler. He
would go on to break the world record in the mile, but for

this day in June of 1965, he and Janell were the returning heroes. When Jim finished second in what would prove to be his last loss for several years, Janell might have begun to feel the pressure too.

In the women's 440 Janell took the lead. I stayed with her and Norma settled a few strides behind us. I coasted into a comfortable pace on the backstretch until about the 330-mark while Janell kept driving in the lead. Norma fell off our pace. When I stepped up my pace to go gradually into an all-out finishing kick, Janell tried to hang on. With about twenty-five yards to go I pulled even with her. She tried to reach back for more, but even as the hometown crowd encouraged her, she ran out of gas. I passed her at the tape, winning with a 54.6. She ran a 54.8 and was terribly disappointed and embarrassed.

Usually I can empathize with a loser, but I try not to feel sorry for them. I must keep the competitive edge, and I always want to win—we all do. But this time, I admit, I felt bad for Janell. "It's not you," she said. "I ran a stupid, foolish race." I didn't wish I hadn't beat her. I just wished that somehow neither of us would have had to lose.

It was true she had not run her own race. And I took a lesson from that. I wanted to remember that when you're favored, and you're encouraged by running before a sympathetic crowd, you still must run a tactical race. You can't just blast off to impress people. Good runners are often just miliseconds apart from each other. A winner will be the one who runs the race that has worked in the past.

In all three of the races overseas, Janell finished first and I finished second. None of the foreign girls beat either of us in any race. I've always wondered if I couldn't have won one or two of those races. Janell and I became close after the Kansas City race, and maybe the edge had been taken off the thrill of winning over her.

Had those races been the finals of the Olympics, I might

have gone for blood and maybe I could have beaten her. But once I realized that we were both ahead of the Europeans, after we had battled all the way, I didn't have that killer instinct left in me. Anyway, I had already beaten her in Kansas City, and I almost regretted it. I'll never know if I could have taken her in Europe. If I had wanted to try it, I had my chance.

When I got back to Cleveland for my senior year in high school, I was welcomed by Madeline Manning Day. There were cheerleaders and a band, and I was supposed to give a little speech. I was all dressed up, and I had written a few notes on a little card. Miss West introduced me and during a standing ovation, I stood at the podium and looked down at my card.

I couldn't see the card! I was so nervous, I couldn't read it. The students kept clapping. I turned to Miss West. "I can't read the card!"

"Well, be calm," she said. "Just do your thing. You'll be fine."

I prayed quickly, "Lord, help me." When the applause subsided the Lord impressed upon me that I should be honest. "I want to tell you something you might think is a little funny," I began. "I had my whole speech on a little card here, but I'm so nervous, I can't read it." It brought down the house, and that relaxed me. I simply told of my experiences in Europe and said I was running for the glory of God. Everything went well. Ever since, I have never done any extensive planning for what I am going to say. I just ask the Lord to help me be honest and to bring the right words to mind. He always does.

The Lord had already begun to heal the relationship between me and my stepfather. Rev. Saulsberry had begun the Mt. Rose Baptist Church, and I helped out a lot. I called on Sunday school children and worked in the church. He was proud that I was becoming well known, and he had been bragging on me at the General Motors plant. Now that I was maturing in my Christian faith and was working for him and for the Lord, we were able to communicate much better.

The Lord had an exciting senior year planned for me in music, track, and church, but not before a few bitter trials.

Chapter Seven

WHO ARE YOU?

With me running more for John Hay (and winning all my races and helping the relay teams win too), the girls' track team won the state championship and advanced to the high school level Amateur Athletic Union Lake Erie competition in Cleveland.

Here I had won the national AAU outdoor quarter-mile title with a girls' division record the year before, and represented the United States in Europe, and had even won the quarter for my age bracket of the University Games in Mexico City in the fall of '65, and now I faced a girl I feared. I had never competed against her before, and to this day I couldn't tell you her name or where she was from. All I know is that I left my strategy on the bus or somewhere. I decided that as strong as I was, the best bet would be to put as much distance as possible between her and me. She was an experienced quarter-miler, so I was going to have to blow her away from the beginning.

I tried. At the halfway point I was several yards ahead and moving well. My experienced opponent was gliding along in second place. I felt I had enough distance between us, but I was beginning to tire quickly—too quickly.

I realized that I had taken off too fast and that I might not have anything left. Rather than being able to gut it out as I had done in the national AAU relay, my psyche worked the other way. Instead of forgetting fatigue and pain and driving through it, I struggled to keep moving.

With 110 yards to go, I heard her moving up directly behind me. My reserves were gone. I kicked my feet as high as I could and pumped my arms, but it felt as if a bear had jumped on my back. I was in a dream with fear chasing me, and I felt weighted down, unable to feel that sweet freedom of movement that had characterized the finishes of my races.

The steps behind me were fast and steady. I felt erratic. I flailed arms and legs as I caught sight of the finish string. We were both running as fast as we could, yet to me the finish line appeared to stay the same distance away. I grimaced, I sucked for air, I set my head straight. With just yards to go she pulled next to me on the right. I fought to maintain position, but at the string she leaned quickly to steal first place.

As I slowed to a stop and dropped my head between my legs to gasp for my recovery, my mind raced as usual. When you've spent yourself physically, your thoughts are almost incoherent. You know whether you've won or lost, and you fight for consciousness to realize what you've won, or what record you've set, or what you've done for your team. This time my thoughts were clear. I knew I had finished second, which would help carry our team to the championship. But I had lost an important battle. I had run a poor race and had been defeated by a peer. It was one thing to finish a few yards behind an Olympian, or a world record holder. But to lose to someone my own age when I held the national division record? *Never again,* I vowed to myself, *will I run that far that fast and let someone beat me by a lean.* I had made the same mistake Janell had made against me in Kansas City. I would not do it again.

During the indoor season under Alex, I found myself one of the team leaders. Of course, after the outdoor nationals the year before and the international competition, I was favored in the quarter mile for the indoor AAU nationals coming up in March of 1966.

Alex had been having trouble finding enough good competition for me and the team, so during the Christmas break he asked Sandra Knott and me to work extra hard (as I had done the year before) and tune up for the Maple Leaf Games in Toronto. "You'll be running the half mile," he said.

"The half?" I asked. "That's Sandra's race, not mine. Let me run the quarter."

"They're not having a quarter up there," he said.

"Then let me run the 220."

"No, run the half. It's just a workout, don't worry about it."

Well, I *was* worried about it. I had run the half mile (880 yards) just once, and that was outdoors. I had won with a time of 2:12, and it wasn't as bad as I thought it might be. But it was grueling. And so what if it was just two quarter miles back to back? That didn't make it any easier. Outdoors it was just twice around a quarter-mile track. Indoors, at the Maple Leaf Games, it would be five times around a tight-banked wooden track against the best half-milers in the world.

By now I knew the track stars of the world. "Will the Russian be there?" I asked. Alex nodded. "And the two from England?" He nodded again. "And the two from Canada?" He kept nodding. "Forget it," I said. "I don't even want to run the half indoors against Sandra."

Alex raised a hand and his eyebrows as he does when he's heard enough and wants to be heard. "It's just a workout, I told you. Don't worry about it. I want you to follow the leader. Whoever takes the lead, probably the Yugoslavian—"

"She's going to be there too?" I asked, rolling my eyes.

Alex ignored me and kept on. "Just follow the leader for as long as you can. It will be a good workout for the indoor nationals."

I didn't much like the idea of losing and being embarrassed by a bunch of internationally experienced half-milers a lot older than me. But it relaxed me to simply remember Alex's advice. "It's just a workout. Follow the leader. Don't worry about it."

On the narrow track in Toronto they lined up all twelve half-milers in a single staggered line. It was a mess. How would we get anywhere? I just let the coach's words echo in my head. I was loose and relaxed, nervous only about the start.

When the gun went off I got my first taste of indoor international competition. I saw girls get bumped hard from both sides, elbowed from the front, stepped on from behind, and have their shorts grabbed briefly (forgive the pun). It scared me so bad I shot to the inside and sprinted into the lead, completely ignoring what Alex had told me. In the lead and sprinting, with almost the whole race still ahead of me—a half mile—I was even more scared.

What are you doing here? I asked myself. *You don't know a good pace for an indoor half. You're not following the leader. You'd better slow down so someone can take the lead and you can do what you were told.* I slacked off the pace a bit and sure enough the Yugoslavian girl passed me near the end of the first lap. *Follow her, follow her, follow her,* I told myself as I slipped in behind and we pounded the boards together. She set her own quick pace and I relaxed in it, wondering if I could have ever gotten around the pack to follow her if I had waited to make my move.

Two laps later she was maintaining a blistering pace, and I was right behind her. The rest of the girls had fallen behind, but I didn't notice. We had passed the halfway point and I was beginning to feel it. I was used to concentrating for a quarter of a mile in competition, but here we were, past that point, with two laps remaining.

As we rounded the far curve, the Yugoslav coach shouted to his runner. "She's getting tired," he said. "Leave her now. Leave her now. Go ahead."

It made me mad. Sure I was tired, but that girl had run just as fast and far as I had. (She was breathing hard, and I knew she was as tired as I was.) And so what if I had run the half mile only once before, and outdoors at that? The Yugoslav girl made a feeble attempt at picking up the pace, and I thought, *That's what you call leaving me? If there's going to be any leaving done, I'll do it.* And I took off.

By the end of the fourth lap I was a good ten yards ahead and from the sound of the footsteps I knew I was pulling away. The crowd was on its feet, the Yugoslav coach was silent, and I had forgotten Alex's advice. As the crowd cheered and cheered I forgot the pain. I leaned into the turns and I heard someone yelling. It sounded as if he were saying "Run as fast as the world record," but it made little sense to me.

I blasted through that final lap as if I were sprinting the 100-yard dash and snapped the tape almost 50 yards ahead. *I'm glad I can go back and tell the coach that I won, but I don't ever want to run the half mile again.* I was surprised and pleased, but when the pain and agony hits, it hits hard. I was congratulated by lots of people as I made my way to the infield to put my sweatsuit back on. I shook my head. *How I hate the half.*

I had hardly had time to realize that I, the youngest girl in the race, and the only high schooler, had beaten some of the best women half-milers in the world. Then a man approached. I didn't notice his microphone. "Who are you?" he asked.

I was sure I was going to be disqualified since I wasn't

really a half-miler. "Well, sir," I said, breathlessly, "my name is Madeline Manning and I'm from Cleveland and I'm really just a quarter-miler who came up here for conditioning. It surprised me that I was even able to keep up with these girls since I've never run the half mile indoors before. My coach said to just stay with the leader, and that's what I was trying to do."

"I can't believe this," he said. "You mean to tell me you've never run the half mile indoors before?"

I nodded as the loud speaker system blared, "Official winning time by Madeline Manning of the Cleveland Track Club is 2:08.4, a new Maple Leaf Games record and a new world indoor record!"

I couldn't believe it. I jumped up and down and screamed and hugged the man. "You didn't know you had broken the world record?" he asked.

"No, nobody told me."

He turned away from me and spoke into his microphone. "Did you hear that, folks? She's broken the world record in the half mile and she's just a quarter-miler."

"Who are you talking to?"

"You're on Canadian television, young lady," he said, laughing. He pointed to a camera. I was so startled I just grabbed up my shoes and sweatsuit and ran right out of the arena. The next day the sports page of the local paper carried a big color photo of me running from the stadium with my shoes and sweatsuit in my arms. The caption read: "Who is she? The girl no one knew broke the world 880-yard record."

"Needless to say, I was the hit of Cleveland and the Cleveland Track Club and John Hay High School. Alex asked, "Now do you want to keep running the half?"

"No," I said. "I want to stay with the 440."

He said okay, but there was a twinkle in his eyes. He knew well that no invitational meet director in his right mind would invite me to a meet for only the quarter when I held the world record for the indoor half. Alex was right. And after I had run the half several more times in competition, Alex entered me for both the quarter and the half and one of the relays in the indoor AAU nationals in Albuquerque, New Mexico.

Since the last indoor nationals, when I was so bitterly disappointed at being left home, I had won the outdoor quarter mile in record time, had run internationally, had won the state high school championship, and had broken the world record in the indoor half. Alex had been so wise. My time had come, and when we arrived in New Mexico, I was favored to win both the quarter and the half and anchor the winning medley relay team.

With about five minutes to go before the quarter-mile trial heats, I was jogging around the handsomely laid out 220-yard indoor track. It was good, new wood, and the distance meant just two laps for a quarter, four laps for a half. It was perfect, and I was ready. I jogged easily into the turn in a final warmup and began to pick up my pace. I wanted to sprint at about three-quarter speed for about a hundred yards, then head for the starting line.

As I swept around the corner and onto the short straightaway, I felt good and loose and ready to beat Charlotte Cook of California. She had an excellent time to her credit, but I had found her not as polite as I thought she should have been. She had been telling everyone that she was going to beat me, which was okay. We all need our psyche games to get ourselves up and maybe get the opponent to start wondering. But when I greeted her she ignored me. And when I tried to be friendly, she was cold. Her strategy was working against her. It was psyching me up. We were going to have a good, entertaining, tough race. But everyone knew who would win. I was in shape and strong. I would not be defeated.

Just three or four more sprinting strides and I would slow up to take off my sweatsuit. Then it happened. I felt a sharp twitch in my right side, and while there was little pain at first, it dropped me to the ground and with the speed I had developed, I rolled over twice and doubled up. Then the pain really hit. I had pulled a muscle in my side, of all places. That's rare, especially for someone who is in shape and warmed up properly. Which I was. There was no explanation for it then, and there isn't now. It was freakish.

The crowd had seen me go down and reacted with a collective groan. I was frantic. I jumped up and tried to tell myself, *It didn't happen. It couldn't have happened.* I tried jogging over to Alex, but I could hardly move. When I got to him I said, "I've pulled a muscle in my side."

He got the qualifying heat postponed for a few minutes and rushed me to the training room where I was given shots to deaden the pain. But the pain remained. I tried jogging again but it felt as if part of my body was going one way and the other part another way. "I don't think I can run, Alex."

"But the doctor said you could run without pain."

"The pain's still there." When I came into the view of the crowd, they gave me a standing ovation and I knew I had to give it a try. "If I get out there on that track, I'm not quitting until I finish," I told Alex.

The qualifying heat began, and I was by far the top runner in the group. They keep the best runners in separate qualifying heats so they don't eliminate each other before the finals. So Charlotte Cook was not in my heat, nor was anyone else who had run the quarter in much less than 60 seconds. After the first ten yards I could hardly stand the pain.

I could hardly do anything. The rest of the girls moved past me, and as I saw them go I noticed that even their pace was terribly slow. The winner would run a 60-second quarter, yet I would finish last. I ran, jogged, limped, cried, held my side, straightened up, doubled over, did everything I could to keep going, as the rest of the pack left me far in the distance.

The pain was almost as bad as the mental anguish, realizing that I was not only not going to qualify for the quarter-mile finals, but I would also likely not run the half or the relays either. I wanted so badly to make up for missing last year's meet and add a good indoor national meet to my recent world record so I could be known as a bona fide world-class runner in more than one event.

As I finished my first lap, the leaders caught me and passed me as they finished their second laps. People were shouting for me to stop and not to hurt myself by continuing. But I would not quit. I staggered another 200 yards or so, but about 20 yards from the finish, that injured muscle gave out completely and I went down in a heap.

Officials and teammates rushed to help me from the track but I swung my elbows and screamed at them, "Don't touch me. I haven't finished yet!" I tried to get to my feet but there was no way. Again they tried to help me, and I again refused. I covered the last several yards on my hands and knees before an ovation I scarcely heard. I was humiliated and disgusted, but I hadn't quit. My time, over two minutes, was not recorded.

Physically, there was little the doctors could do for me. They laid me out in the training room and simply said that I would have to be wrapped and would have to rest the pulled muscle until it healed, probably a matter of several weeks. There would be no half mile, no relays in this meet. I was so hurt and frustrated that I couldn't even cry.

"You have to cry," Sandra Knott told me, as everyone else left the room. And when the tears finally started, she left too. I was alone and humiliated and angry. I took out my rage on the room. Still holding my side, with my free hand I slammed tables and chairs around until there was little more I could do. I slumped to the floor, sobbing, and they wisely left me alone for several more minutes. I had worked so hard, practiced so long. I was beginning to realize how much competing meant to me.

What was I angry about? Fate? Luck? Was God trying to tell me something? Maybe to slow down and get my priorities straight? I had not been studying my Bible regularly but felt close to him. And I had been helping out in my stepfather's church. I did a lot of hard thinking as I healed over the next several weeks.

During the summer of '66 I looked high and low for a meet with a quarter mile for women. It seemed no one was running them any more. If I wanted to run, I had to run the half. It never hit me that my world record might have had something to do with that. But the pace of a summer of traveling and competing had caught up with me. What began as stomach cramps landed me in the hospital with a viral infection and a week of tests.

By the last few days, I was ready to get going. I was still weak, but I tried to stay in shape by running up and down the halls. "You don't need to be here," the nurses would say, "we'll get you out soon."

"You'd better," I said. "I've got to run in the nationals." They'd smile and nod, not really believing I would be running. But I knew I would. I had to. I was going to run my new specialty, the half mile, the race I had run all summer. And against Charlotte Cook, no less.

Two days after I got out of the hospital I flew to Virginia, where I was supposed to be picked up and taken to Maryland. After a mixup and a delay of several hours, I finally arrived in Maryland just after midnight on the day I would run in the qualifying heat and the semifinal, if I qualified. I did well in both races between eating and sleeping, but the 90-degree heat and 80 percent humidity were taking their toll. I slept heavily and woke up weak the next day. I knew Charlotte would be fresh. She had run well and looked strong in her heat and semi.

Her strategy, I learned later, was to run the first quarter mile in 65 seconds, an easy pace. Then she planned to pick it up and finish with a 60-second last quarter. My strategy was the opposite. I wanted to put some distance between myself and the rest of the field with a 60-second first quarter and then hang onto the lead, even if it meant running the second quarter slower.

That's exactly what happened. At one point I had about a 20-yard lead on Charlotte, but at the end of the first quarter mile, I had run a 61.0 and she had run a 65.0. She caught me coming around the last curve and we battled all the way down the backstretch. She took the lead by a step, then I moved back into the lead. Back and forth, back and forth. I felt dead, and the crowd was loving the race.

With five yards to go I gave it everything I had and leaned toward the tape. She outleaned me.

I was disappointed to lose, but I had done my best. "Girl, that was really a good race," I said, gasping.

"Thanks. I hear you were in the hospital or something?"

"Yeah. I just got out the day before yesterday."

"Well, I don't want to run against you when you're well!"

Chapter Eight

TIGERBELLE

Mr. Edward Temple didn't want any losers on his Tennes-
see State University women's track and field team. What an
honor to be a Tigerbelle!

I had been aware of the Tigerbelles ever since I had
begun running nationally. When they stepped onto the
track, most other athletes just stared. Some whispered, "It's
the Tigerbelles. The Tigerbelles are here." The Tigerbelles
looked proud and tough in blue and white. And they were.

Now I was one. Madeline Manning, Tigerbelle.

The track team members roomed together, and my
roommate, Una Morris of Jamaica, was as happy as I was
that my mother stayed with us the first week. Una was
away from her country for the first time, so it was good to
have a mom around for awhile.

Mr. Temple showed the Tigerbelles around campus and
laid some ground rules for us. He also helped us with our
class schedules, advising us to not overdo, and to keep
every afternoon open between three and five. We were
there on scholarships, and for our education, room, and
board, we owed Tennessee State those two hours a day,
plus the meets. Oh, those two hours a day!

Almost every Tigerbelle came from a track club where she had been the star. We were singularly unimpressed with each other. You could go off during the summer and break a world record, only to come back to Tennessee State where someone would say, "Oh, really? I'll bet I could beat you." (And she probably could!)

In our own way this drew us together as a team. We were jealous of each other's accomplishments, but we respected each other's dedication and sacrifice. And we pulled for each other because good individual performances meant team victories. And we were all proud to be Tigerbelles. We were running in the shadows of such superstars as Willye White, Wilma Rudolph, and Martha Watson. Olympians Edythe McGuire and Wyomia Tyus were still there. We looked to them as big sisters.

Besides them, there were no star Tigerbelles, because we were all stars. While I stood out in high school and everyone made sure I got home from parties early so I could rest, no one at Tennessee State seemed to care. The campus was crawling with track stars who could get involved in anything they wanted, and everyone else took it in stride. If I went to a party and wanted to stay half the night, no one treated me like royalty or worried that I should be home in bed. I was just one of the girls.

There were so many parties and activities and studies that I found myself reading my Bible less and less. I know I have to be "in the Word" if I want to grow in the Lord and be an effective witnessing Christian. But there was too much going on. I was working too hard. I was too tired. I was too . . . too anything. I just flat let my time with the Lord slip away. And I paid for it eventually, too.

I was glad Alex had been a tough coach and had made me run cross-country twice each year, otherwise I'd never have been able to take the workouts Mr. Temple directed. I had heard about The Hill from former Tigerbelles, but the first time I ran it, I couldn't believe it. Mr. Temple wanted it to get easier and easier for us, so he started us running with a weight in each hand.

Actually The Hill was several hills, all on the same three-and-a-half-mile course. We began by running almost straight up for about 100 yards. Just when our legs tightened and we could hardly pull any more, the course leveled off for a few yards. Our legs would recover and we'd start to pick up our pace a little and another hill would loom over the horizon. After several small hills we came to a huge downward slope that took ten minutes to run down. After all the chugging up and down, the decline was easier to run and gave us a false sense of relaxation.

When the course leveled off again we realized how tired we were and how the coasting hadn't really rested or relaxed us at all. It just postponed the pain. Then it was a long straight stretch until we hit a pasture. I ran through the pasture and around the Cumberland River, while the other girls (because they were sprinters, not middle-distance runners) cut across and rested, waiting for me. When I got back from the river, Mr. Temple would say, "Manning's here now. Let's go." Then it was back to where we started. You can imagine how long that hill was going up, if it was ten minutes coming down. I'd like to have died. By the time I got to the top I could hardly move, but we had to run around the agricultural building with all its smelly animals making noises at us as we ran by. Finally we got back to the track. It was terrible.

Of course, world-class runners learn to endure. And that Hill has separated a lot of women and girls. The women became national and international champs and the Tigerbelles became winners, while the girls who couldn't take it packed their bags.

After several weeks of running The Hill I felt as strong as I'd ever been. Once I ran the more than three miles in just over fifteen minutes. I was frustrated, though. I felt Mr. Temple wasn't coaching me properly. Because he'd never had a bona fide quarter-miler and half-miler before, he was coaching me like a sprinter, only harder and at longer distances. Finally I went to his office and I told him.

"I know, Madeline, and I'm sorry," he said. He had seemed cold to me, totally the opposite of Alex. "But since I've never had distance runners before, I'm feeling my way. You need my help in improving your speed. Maybe you can help me learn how to coach distance running."

We talked about other things too, and I came to really appreciate Mr. Temple. He wasn't cold at all. He was a hard, demanding coach, but he cared. (He still follows my career and is proud of my accomplishments.) I suggested he contact Alex for more hints on how to coach distance runners. Meanwhile, The Hill had made me tough and hard for 1967, and I was ready for four important meets: the AAU indoor and outdoor nationals and the biggies, the Pan-American Games in Toronto and the Europe vs. Americas Games in Montreal. I'd never been to the Pan-American Games, but they were all the Tigerbelles seemed to talk about. Being the year before the Olympics, the '67 Games would be all-important. I began to really look forward to them. They made the Olympics seem more than just a dream.

At the indoor nationals in New York I found myself nervous and excited, though I had been there before. I won, but the biggest impression on me was that everyone seemed to be looking ahead to the Pan-American Games. It became more and more obvious how important that competition would be to everyone's Olympic hopes. I had been told that when Olympic fever hits you'll see athletes coming out of the walls for every event. Old-timers, young upstarts—everyone wants to run for the gold. Every event is flooded with talent. It started at the indoor nationals, and I figured by the time the Pan-Ams rolled around, I'd really see who had their eyes on Mexico City for '68.

I didn't have to wait until the Pan-Ams, as it turned out. At the outdoor nationals in Los Angeles during the summer, where I was again a winner, Olympic fever really hit. It was tune-up-for-Toronto time, and then who knows—? I was part of it. Not taking anyone for granted, not even those coming out of retirement, I still felt fortunate because I would be just twenty years old during the Olympics. Age and shape would not be liabilities. If I had it in me at all, I had no excuse not to excel.

I won a gold medal in a relay at the Pan-American Games and immediately began looking ahead to the Europe vs. Americas Games in Montreal. It was to be the best from Europe against the best from North America, South America, Central America and the Latin Americas. I could hardly wait. If I could beat Vera Nikolic of Yugoslavia, I might be the favorite at Mexico City in the Olympics. Most of all, I would have confidence that I could beat anyone in the world. Vera was the best woman 800-meter runner in all of Europe.

On the night of the meet it seemed that even the other athletes were waiting for our event. It would be the race of the evening. The crowd buzzed about it, and I grew more and more tense as the meet wore on. Occasionally I would cross Vera's path on the infield and we would both put on casual faces as if we were tough, not worried, not even concerned. But I was scared to death. Once I saw her when she didn't see me. She looked scared too. I was so relieved. *You're as scared as I am*, I thought. *How about that? You're not as tough as you think you are.*

But she *was* tough, as I was to learn. I looked over at Alex on the sidelines. He smiled and raised his fist at me, mouthing, "That's my girl." I was elated. He knew me, he believed in me. I was going to win this race—for Alex, for Mama, for me, for God.

71

When the gun sounded I forgot everything but the fluidity of my running motion. I shot away from the pack and flashed around the first curve. I noticed the stars and the blackness of the cool night, but I didn't realize how fast I was going. Lee Evans, a close friend and a star on the men's team, ran across the infield and shouted from the inside as I breezed through the 220-yard mark, "Slow down! Slow down!" He turned to no one in particular and threw up his hands. "She's running too fast!"

But I felt no pain. I was gliding. It was as if I were in animation, floating in slow motion. I knew I was really moving, but I felt like liquid personified. There was nothing, no one but me and God.

Coming out of the curve and onto the straight I was suddenly myself again. I heard footsteps behind me closing the gap, and I knew it had to be Vera. But I felt so good. Vera was not a concern to me. I led as the field moved into the final lap. On the backstretch I again slipped into total relaxation, and while I knew the other girls were not far behind, I heard nothing but my own breathing and my feet clipping away at the track.

Usually at the 600-yard mark or so I begin to feel tightness or at least fatigue and pain. I knew I would feel it later, but now I felt nothing. I was maintaining a torrid pace and no doubt could have run a world record. As I moved out of the last curve I reminded myself what Mr. Temple had taught me about the finishing kick. *Lift your knees higher and higher with each step. Move slowly into a full sprint.*

My speed was the best it had ever been, so owning the lead and just starting to build toward my sprinting finish, I knew the race was mine. I heard Vera closing fast, pounding away, running that classic European strategy: staying in the pack until near the end and then finishing strong. (Some Americans have a reputation for going out fast and leaving nothing for the end.) Vera pulled up behind me and began to move to my outside. I wasn't worried. I still felt no pain. I was strong and began to lift my knees higher and higher. I was near my flat-out top speed when Vera inched next to me.

Now I would hold my form and blast away from her. As I was in mid-stride, with my right arm back, Vera drove her left elbow into my ribs, blasting pain through my torso and spilling me into the infield, where I rolled over on hands and knees. My body screamed with pain, and the fatigue and oxygen debt that had built up over nearly a half mile washed through me. I ignored it and scrambled to my feet, jumping back onto the track, sprinting with every ounce of strength I could steal from my limbs. And I hated Vera.

With arms and legs flying, I caught her so fast that both of us nearly froze. I was stunned, and I could see by the look on her face that she was too. With twenty yards to go, we were both spent. The rest of the field was far behind, and the fans jumped to their feet to shriek us home. Grimacing, reaching, charging, we struggled neck and neck to the finish, where I outleaned her by a fraction.

I was nearly delirious, but as I ran through, a man grabbed me around my waist, knocking the wind from me. "Are you okay?" he asked. Lee Evans yelled, "Leave her alone! Put her down!" But when he did I blacked out. Lee and some of my teammates helped me try to walk. (Stopping after a long hard race is like running your system into a brick wall. You have to keep moving.)

I was finally able to walk on my own and to jog a little, but breathing was difficult. They took me to the training room, where I believe God judged me for hating Vera, even for an instant. I lay down and tried to tell the trainers I needed air, but they just kept talking about what a slug I had taken from Vera. When I was stretched out on the table, my muscles collapsed and I passed out again. I was in shock, and the Canadian doctor worked quickly to get me to breathe. When I was semiconscious, he instructed me to breathe very slowly.

Pain flooded my body with each breath. When I was breathing on my own, everyone left me alone in the room. I cried. Sure, Vera had been wrong and should have been disqualified for an obvious foul. But was a race, a victory, so important it was worth hating someone? The Lord impressed upon me that a material victory meant nothing. "Haven't I brought you this far?" he seemed to ask me. "Couldn't you trust me to help you without hating someone just to win?"

I felt terrible. It was as if he were chastising me, and I knew I deserved it. I was getting a spiritual whipping. Suddenly I was nauseated and had to get to the bathroom. As I tumbled to my hands and knees from the pain, I was hit with a wave of diarrhea. Crawling to the bathroom, I prayed, "Lord, forgive me. Get me out of this and I'll never do that again." Within minutes I was as good as gold. I was still weak and had a headache, but I was able to walk out on my own to get my medal.

I stood on the victory stand with Vera on my right and a German girl (who had finished third) on my left. I had lost my hatred for Vera. I reached to her. "That was an excellent race," I said. She ignored my hand and grunted, turning her back to me. The German girl quickly came to my defense, leaning across the victory stand and scolding Vera in broken English.

"You have your nerve," she said. "They should have disqualified you for what you did. She won fair and square and you should shake her hand. They posted the finish picture and it clearly shows that she won, even after you knocked her off the track. She beat you, that's all. She just beat you."

The German, running third, had been in a perfect place to see exactly what had happened. If Vera had been disqualified, the German would have finished second. But she seemed most upset by Vera's poor sportsmanship. Vera hung her head and cried.

I think we both learned a lesson that night. And when I had time to think about it, I realized that I had beaten the other best 800-meter runner in the world, and that I could have beaten her much more easily and by a bigger margin, had the race been run fairly. *You've got a chance,* I told myself. *You could win the olympic gold at Mexico City.*

Chapter Nine

NIGGER

I was in the training room being treated for a muscle pull during the fall of my sophomore year at Tennessee State when a football player came in from practice and asked the trainer who I was.

"That's a girl from your home state, John," the trainer said.

"Is that Madeline Manning from Cleveland?" John Linder Jackson asked. (He was from Columbus.) "I've heard a lot about her."

I was introduced to the big, wide, strong bronze man, but I chose to ignore him for several weeks. I could tell he was interested in me, but I had too much to think about, and I guess he just didn't interest me that much. The Olympics were coming up the next summer, and a romance was something I needed like a broken leg.

If there *was* a football player I was interested in, it was Number 85, the one I watched from my window in the women's residence center. Ooh, 85 was something else. I'd call my roommates, Lottie Thompson from Detroit and Una, over to the window. "Look at this guy play ball," I'd say, never taking my eyes from the practice field. "Isn't he something?" Una and Lottie would smile and shake their heads at me. Their poor dumb roommate was developing a crush on a football player with no name—only a number.

But he was so graceful. "He plays like a ballerina," I'd say, not realizing that Una and Lottie had already left the window. Number 85 was the biggest, the fastest, the most adept pass catcher, obviously a star. "I'm gonna go to the next game and watch him play," I said.

At the next game, Number 85 caught everything thrown near him and scored three touchdowns. I left my girlfriends when the game was over so I could get down to where the players left the stadium. I hoped he'd have his helmet off so I could see who he was. He did, and I did. Who should it be but John Linder Jackson!

I quit ignoring him, and we soon began dating. If impressive athletic ability seems a weak base for love, you may be onto the reason our eventual marriage never worked out. I was proud to be seen with John, and in 1968 we were engaged. But marriage was out of the question during the Olympic year.

After a highly successful winter and early spring at the indoor nationals, several tune-up meets, the outdoor nationals in Sacramento, and the Olympic trials in Pomona, I was ready to head for Los Alamos, New Mexico, with the rest of the U.S. team for training camp. Before I left, however, I started getting phone calls.

"What makes you think a nigger can beat white girls in the half mile?" an anonymous caller would ask. "It isn't a nigger's event." Hate mail came too. I threw it away and prayed about it, but I was still scared. No American woman, let alone a black woman, had ever won a medal in the Olympics in a distance event. Here I was, the only black in a field of mostly Europeans, running what was then the longest race in the Games for women.

I thought I had a good shot at the gold, but I felt

doubtful stares from all over. John was concerned about the effect of the mail and phone calls. My mother was hopeful, but I knew it was just because she was Mother, not because she really knew anything about international track.

Alex decided I should put all my eggs in one basket and ignore the 400-meter competition, even though I qualified for that event too. It made me feel that he thought I could win the gold in the 800, and that was what was important. He was the only one I could really talk to about my hopes for a gold medal, because everyone else reacted so strangely. It was as if they thought I was just dreaming, that I could never handle the pressure. I thought I was in a perfect position, being young and strong and in shape and having run so much internationally at my age. Who in the world did they think was supposed to beat me? They must have thought I would beat myself by choking under pressure. And that was insulting.

No one seemed to know where I was coming from. Even Mr. Temple, though he was working with me and knew that I had it in me physically, had trouble hiding his doubts. He wouldn't admit it to this day, I'm sure, but I think the overwhelming odds against a young black American girl beating the European women in an event they had dominated for years got to him too.

Feeling rather alone in my quest, and having to go to training camp several days before Alex, the only man who really believed in me, I left for New Mexico. The most crucial part of our training in '68 was altitude acclimation. Mexico City was several thousand feet above sea level and would put the Americans at a tremendous disadvantage unless we could get used to running where the air was thinner.

After a week of walking and jogging in New Mexico, we were taken into the mountains where it was well over seven thousand feet, higher even than Mexico City would be.

Until Alex arrived, I was to run with Doris Brown of Seattle and another teammate, Francie Kraker. We were to work under Doris's coach.

Doris was a Christian, so we had more in common than running. She was a toughie to compete against. More than once I had learned that when Doris was competing, I had to go out with her from the beginning and stay close enough to outsprint her at the end. She didn't have great speed, but she had endurance that could wear out almost anyone. I swear she could run a 1500-meter pace for ten miles.

I really enjoyed Doris, but I did have a falling out with her coach. When we got to the higher elevation, we were to run a three-mile course through the foothills in the mountains and then come back on the same route for a total of six miles. The first day we were instructed to take it easy. Trying to run all out at that altitude before becoming acclimated to it could really hurt a runner.

Francie and Doris and I jogged the first mile and half or so; then we walked, collecting rocks and arrowhead material we found along the way. When we returned with all our loot, it was obvious we hadn't worked too hard. But then, that wasn't the point; we knew the workouts would get tougher. I was running in the afternoons too, so I was getting plenty of work anyway.

The next day we did more running and less walking, but I didn't try to match Doris's pace. I had my endurance down pat and I felt I needed more speed work, which I was getting in my afternoon work. I didn't lag back too far, and I didn't loaf, but neither did I try to run the course hard, like Doris. And Francie wasn't capable of that pace anyway.

For some reason, Doris's coach thought I was loafing, and he called Alex. Alex called me later that night. I was furious. "I'm working," I told him. "You know me well enough to know that. Did he call Francie's coach too?"

"No, he was just concerned about you. Don't worry about it. I know you work hard. I just wanted to hear your side."

It was impossible to sleep. I tossed and turned, determined to show Doris's coach some hard running, if that was what he wanted. In the morning I was already outside when Doris and Francie came out. "You're up mighty early," they said.

"I sure am. You guys ready for some running this mornin'?"

"*You* sure sound ready."

"I am."

I had been sleeping in the van on the way to the course each morning, but not today. I sat with my arms folded over my windbreaker and sweatsuit. I was ready. When we arrived I peeled down to just my track suit. The other girls left their sweats and windbreakers on as usual. "Let's get going," I said. "It's cold out here." And I took off like I was running a 100-yard dash. The other girls finally caught up with me but I kept pushing the pace, nearly running them into the ground. I was the strongest middle-distance runner in the world. If I had to prove it, I would.

By the time I finished the first half of the course, Francie had stopped twice and Doris had fallen far off the pace. I jogged in circles and ran in place waiting for them. When they arrived Francie said, "Are you crazy? What the hell are you doing? I can't keep up."

"I can't run that hard either," Doris said. "I don't feel good today."

"You can stay here for all I care," I said. "I'm heading back. And off I ran again, covering the last half of the course faster than the first. I arrived back at the van a full fifteen minutes before Doris and Francie.

"You're back fast," Doris's coach said.

"I went out fast and I came back fast," I said stonily. On the way back in the van Doris said, "Madeline, don't even think about moving up to long distance running. I'd never have a chance against you." I never heard another word about loafing or needing more work.

On the way to Mexico City, I had time to think about the upcoming Games. They could be the highlight of my athletic career, or they could be the most disappointing days of my life. Besides the fear of the pressure and the competition and the international exposure via television, I couldn't shake the fear that one of my hate-mail writers or the threatening callers might be out to get me in Mexico City.

To them I was a nigger who had no business in a white woman's event. I hadn't even known what a nigger was until as a child I went one day with my mother to a white section of Cleveland where she did housework. I had been playing with the neighborhood kids for more than an hour when one mother screamed at her daughter to get away from me. She grabbed her and spanked her in front of everyone as if she had contaminated herself by being near me. I felt cheap and dirty, but I knew I wasn't.

That made me aware of my blackness, but *nigger* was not a word I ever accepted. *Nigger* meant something different than being black. It meant being low and despicable and stupid and lazy. And if there are niggers in this world, a lot of them are white. I vowed then that one day I would be something, somebody who could change things so Mother wouldn't have to clean white people's homes. If it meant going to college and being a professor or even a doctor, I would do it. I didn't know my avenue to success would be track and music. I just knew I would change things for Mother.

Mexico City would be my opportunity, as never before and maybe since, to be somebody, to run for the glory of God and to make Mother proud too. She would be there, and I could think of nothing to make her happier than seeing me prove myself as the class of the world in the 800-meter run. I wanted to win the gold and break the world record.

I'll never forget the opening ceremonies for the '68 Olympiad. I had been in big, full stadiums before, but they were never like this. The colors, the noise, the spirit, the joy, the international flavor. The Olympic Village had athletes in uniforms of every color, from every nation. I forgot the danger I had felt before, but the nagging fear of failure remained deep within me. I dreaded the actual running. There would be qualifying heats, then semifinals, then the finals. If I made it that far.

During the parade I tried not to think of the competition but rather I tried to drink in the flavor of the whole scene. I knew I'd never be able to forget it even if I'd wanted to, but I wanted more. I wanted to consciously record every sight and sound and smell. It was exhilarating. I wondered if winning the gold would be as exciting as the opening ceremonies. Would just being here be enough to satisfy me if indeed I was in over my head and had to settle for less than first place?

I worked out with my teammates every day, and we found ourselves more subdued and less talkative as our individual races approached. When I dwelt on the race, I almost panicked. Yet I had to think about it. I had to strategize, to calm myself, to remind myself of my shape, my training, my coach, my ability, my background, my standing in the world. I was the best. All I had to do was prove it.

I began spending more time talking myself into a calmer state about the races than in worrying about them. I wanted to do my best. I didn't want to choke under the pressure. The other 800-meter girls had to be just as worried and unsure of themselves. Why couldn't I lead the way, be the calmest, train the hardest, be the most prepared? I would be.

The qualifying heats would be easy, but I was as nervous before mine as I would be in the semis. I had never been to the Olympics before. What if I tripped, or pulled a muscle, or was bumped, or just couldn't handle the tension? There would be no tomorrow unless I finished among the first in my heat. I just had to qualify for the next step toward the gold.

Once the race was underway I settled down. The stadium was full, though we were still three days away from the finals. The crowd was cheering for everyone, but I'm sure each competitor thought it was for her alone. As the best runners are relegated to separate heats so they don't eliminate each other before the finals, I found my qualifier rather easy and breezed in. The semifinal would be more difficult, mainly because of one person. Vera Nikolic had qualified in another heat and would face me in the semis. I didn't know whether to look forward to it or not.

Even if she beat me I would qualify for the finals, but what if she tried knocking me off the track again? How should I run against her? Should I run away from her, or let her take the lead? Should I ignore her and just run my race? Should I box her in so she wouldn't even qualify for the final and I would have one less world-class runner to worry about? I worried about it until race time.

I was terribly nervous as we left the tunnel on the way to the track, and if it hadn't been for a Cleveland newspaperman stopping me, I might not have had what it took to qualify. I'll never know. All I know is, he made me mad—mad enough to do my best. I was last in line, and he held me up.

"Madeline," he said, "you know a lot of people back in Cleveland are watching you, and they're thrilled that you've made it even this far. Do you think you're going to make it through this semifinal?"

What a question! Here I was, ready to go to the track, and

he was asking me if I thought I could make it through the race. It was as if he were saying, you've already done all anyone in Cleveland would have expected. I was hurt and angry.

"Look," I said, "everybody who comes to the Olympics comes to win, and I'm no different. I'm sure not going out there to lose. I'm going to qualify right now, and I'm going to win the finals." And I marched away, fighting tears.

No one understood, no one cared. No one thought I could do it, and they weren't even hoping I would. "Lord," I prayed silently, "I know I haven't been in the Word as much as I should, but I want you to know that I am running for your glory, not for Mother's or Dad's or mine or Alex's. I am running for you."

As we stood at our marks, I remembered that Vera was in the race. I shot a quick glance her way. She looked nervous and upset and was not even trying to hide it. She was psyching no one, but I figured I'd better keep her in mind, because she'd be dogging my steps all the way. Her country had won not one medal in all the competition, and she was their last hope. Not only did she have to qualify, but she had to place among the top three in the finals for a medal. She had as much pressure as any of us.

The anger and isolation started my adrenalin pumping, and I took the lead from the start. I was running easily and strong and felt good. When I finished the first lap, I knew I was going to qualify for the finals. There's nothing like that feeling. I just knew I could hold my pace, and even if a couple of runners passed me, I had enough left to finish among the qualifiers for the finals. Then I began wondering about Vera. I glanced around. My lead was secure, but Vera wasn't even second. I couldn't afford to keep looking behind me, but I took one more long glance as I moved into the last curve. No Vera. She wasn't going to challenge me for the lead. *She must be just running hard enough to barely qualify and is saving herself for the final,* I told myself.

But I was wrong. As I crossed the finish line I turned

around and looked through all the runners and Vera wasn't there. Doris Brown, waiting to run in the next heat, had watched our race. "What happened to Vera?" I asked her, puffing. Then I noticed some of Vera's teammates crying. "What's wrong with everybody, Doris?"

"I don't know, Mad," Doris said. "Vera stopped after 300 meters and just walked off the track and right out of the stadium."

I could hardly believe it. I knew she'd had a lot of pressure, but she was too tough an athlete to quit a race. No one knew what had happened or why. That night I learned that her coach had followed her out of the stadium and up to the footbridge that connected the practice track and the stadium. He saw her climbing the fence on the bridge and caught her just before she tried to jump to her death.

It really shook me up. I wanted badly to see her, but they were not letting her talk to anyone. We prayed for her, and it was all everyone talked about the next day, an off day for the track and field athletes. I tried to put it out of my mind because the final was coming up, but it was impossible. Here was a sad girl with a ton of pressure who not only let down herself and her country and her coach, but who had nowhere to turn for strength. The pressure of international competition was too much, and she had come to the end of herself. I wished there was something I could do for her.

Images flashed through my mind of the first time I had seen her. After reading her name and following her times in the newspaper, I had been scared of her in Canada at the Europe vs. Americas Games. She had looked so tough, so together, so in shape. And I remembered how self-confident and sure she looked until I caught her with her guard down. That was when I knew she was as nervous as I was. That was when she was at the top of the world in her event, and I wondered if my beating her by a hundredth of a second had started her downfall.

Chapter Ten

The FINALS

The next day, as I left the Olympic Village to go for the 800-meter finals with Doris (she too had qualified), we noticed Vera with her coach. She was crying. I left the other girls and ran to her.

"How are you feeling?" I asked. She didn't speak much English, but she shrugged and nodded, trying to hold back her tears. I took her hands in mine, and though I knew she wouldn't understand every word, I hoped she'd understand where I was coming from. She looked amazed that I would break my concentration on the finals just to talk to her. "I know that you are a great athlete," I said. "I want to see you go back and get yourself together and get your mind together. Pray to God for strength, and when you come back, you'll come out fighting and be the runner I know you are." She cried openly then and nodded as we hugged each other.

(A year later at the Europe vs. Americas Games in Germany I ran into Vera's coach. "How is she?" I asked. "She's here," he told me. "When you stopped to talk to her before your own finals, it brought tears to my eyes. If you hadn't done that, I'm sure she would have given up. It was the turning point in her life. She's back in training, and while she's not in top shape yet, she's coming back." By then she had seen me and ran up to hug me. Three years later in Munich she was again among the top five 800-meter women in the world.)

On the practice track I was so nervous I was exhausted. I told Doris that if she stayed with me, we could get first and second place. "We've got to go to the front, and if you're out there with me, I know you can hold off the rest of those girls with your endurance." She nodded, but something was wrong. I figured she was just nervous. "We can't get caught in the pack," I reminded her. "We'll get boxed in and jostled, and in this kind of competition, that will be the race." She didn't respond, and I went for my rubdown from Alex.

I was tight and tired and panicky. Alex knelt over me in the infield of the practice track and softly discussed strategy as his fingers bit into my leg and arm and back muscles. He was reassuring with his fatherly manner and his Hungarian accent. I appreciated him so much. I wanted to win for him, just because of all the hours and years he had put into my career while asking nothing.

I wanted to win for Mother, because she was there to see me and because this was my way of making her proud. I wasn't a professor or a doctor, but I wasn't what those phone calls and letters said I was either. And neither was she. I wanted to win for John. And most of all, I would be running for Jesus.

"There will be no time for jockeying for position," Alex was saying as my breathing evened out and I shut my eyes. He massaged away. "If you get a good lane, watch your pace and the other girls and be among the leaders when you cut over (international rules required that we run in our own lanes for the first 100 meters before breaking to the inside). Run your own race, but don't get boxed in, and don't worry about anyone else."

The race was just fifteen minutes away, but I actually fell into a nervous sleep. Alex rubbed me loose and kept talking, and I realized that he was almost as jittery as I was. Here was his chance to coach a medalist, maybe even a gold medalist. Then came the announcement for 800-meter finalists to come into the stadium. I still get nervous just thinking about it. In the pit of my stomach was a feeling of flat-out fear. Not just jumpiness, not just butterflies. Fear.

As we eight finalists waited in the tunnel in our sweat suits, getting assigned numbers, an English girl kept trotting in front of me and glaring at me. It was as if she were saying, "If I get no one else, I'll get you, Manning." I was thinking, *Why don't you just sit down and rest?*

At first I thought it was just my imagination, but then she did it again. And again. I smiled at her; she scowled. I'll never know why, but it hit me as the funniest thing. Maybe that was her way of showing the tension, but I couldn't get over it. I started to giggle to myself, thinking how hilarious it was for someone to act that way in the finals of the Olympics when we were all past the point of being psyched. We were all scared, all jittery. No one needed to act tough.

And then she did it again. I couldn't help myself. I threw my head back and laughed and laughed. I couldn't stop. I roared, and when the other girls saw me, they laughed too. The English girl thought I was crazy, but one thing was certain: she wasn't going to psych me with that dirty look business.

Alex paced back and forth. "I'm glad you can laugh at a time like this," he said, looking like he was at a funeral.

They herded us into chutes, which took off a bit of the tension. I felt like a horse being guided into the starting gate. I was assigned lane eight, the worst possible lane. That meant I would start on the far outside, and with a staggered start (each lane out starts further up the track),

I would run the first 100 meters with everyone behind me, and I wouldn't be able to tell if I was running too fast or too slow or what.

As we approached the line, I heard bongo drums and a bunch of Jamaicans chanting, "Madeline!" It shocked me, and I stared into the distance to see where it was coming from. I spotted the drummers, and there was Una. She was there as a sprinter from the Jamaican team and had put these guys up to chanting for me. For a second I forgot all about the race.

The combination of having seen Vera, advising Doris on strategy, getting a rubdown and instructions from Alex, laughing at the "starting gate" and at the English girl, and having bongo drummers call my name, kept me from dwelling on the race to the point where I would have tied myself in knots. But the fun part wasn't over yet.

The official starters in the Olympics are always from the host countries and we foreign runners have to be briefed on the language enough to know when he is telling us to strip down, take our marks, and get set for the gun. Well, there were no Spanish girls in the 800 finals, so we were all listening very intently and watching each other to make sure we didn't miss anything he said or did. He shouted one command and we all looked at him and each other. To make it easier for us to understand, he moved into a pantomime that broke us up again. As he repeated his instruction, he pretended to wiggle out of a sweat suit. We got the point, and soon we were on the track awaiting the gun.

The weirdest thing happened when I heard the gun. I was afraid I wouldn't know where everyone else was, so I started very fast to assure myself of being in a good position when the time came for us to break to the inside. It seemed as if I had stayed at the starting line and was watching myself from behind. I could see the whole race, even the girls behind me. I knew I was really moving and that I was way ahead, and I was able to tell myself to slacken the pace a bit and save something for the end. I didn't want to run a foolish race just because I was nervous and then find out I was exhausted (and passed by everyone else) at the end.

I had never had the sensation before, and I've never had it since. It wasn't like the slow-motion, animated feeling I had had in the race against Vera in Canada. It was more as if I had left my body and could see everything from where I started. I didn't know what to make of it.

When we cut to the inside in the middle of the first curve, I found myself way out ahead. After having warned Doris to try to stay with me and not get boxed in by the Russian, I thought I had better slacken my pace even a little more. When I heard Doris behind me I moved to the outside so she could have the inside lane. But when she came up next to me I realized it wasn't Doris. It was a Rumanian girl.

I knew good and well that Doris had enough speed to catch me at the pace I was running, so I figured she must be ignoring our agreed-upon strategy. I was irritated. Here I had altered my pace and even made room for her, and she had chosen to use another strategy. *Forget it,* I told myself. *You might as well run your own race. If the U.S. doesn't get one and two, it won't be your fault.* I began to pick up the pace again, and the Rumanian girl stayed with me on the inside. It could be that the thirty or forty yards of easy pacing I had done helped me conserve my strength, but, whatever the reason, I felt unusually strong at the end of the first 400 meters. The rest of the field was not far behind us two leaders, and the crowd was enjoying it. In my nervousness and under the pressure, I felt no pain.

It seemed as if I could just take off and leave the Rumanian, but good sense took over. *You'd better wait,* I told myself. *At least until you get around that first curve of the second lap. It may just be the excitement telling you that you can run away from this field, so save yourself. Save yourself.*

By now, of course, all of us had worked up a good sweat. As we came out of that first curve on the second lap, I got a whiff of the strangest odor, and I could hardly stand it. I frankly don't know if it was the Rumanian, whose different food tastes might have caused an unusual perspiration odor, or if it was just something in the infield. Whatever it was, I wanted to get away from it. It was time to make my move anyway because the rest of the field was closing the gap. The smell was like garlic and a mixture of other exotic food, and I said, *My Lord,* and took off. *I want to get this thing over with.*

I slowly built up to a full sprint. By the middle of the backstretch, with 200 meters to go, I was pulling away from everyone. I settled into a high-knee action drive, and it was then that I realized the gold medal would be all mine.

With 80 meters to go I had a good 10-meter lead and I wanted to maintain my pace to save one big kick for the end.

Madeline, I said to myself, *you are runnin' this thing by yo'self!* I didn't even think about the time until I had about 10 meters to go and heard someone say, "Break two minutes!"

I had saved my strength until the end, but being so far ahead, I had not thought to push it in. I gave one final burst of speed but missed breaking two minutes by nine-tenths of a second. My winning time of 2:00.9 was a new Olympic and world record, and all I could hear was Mama. Above all those screaming people I could hear her voice. "Thank you, Jesus! Thank you, Lord!" She just kept praising.

Somehow Alex fought his way out of the stands and onto the field. He was crying. I was in a daze. It had hardly hit me yet. When I got my sweats on I found Doris, and it all came back to me that she had ignored our strategy. "What happened to you?" I asked.

She was crying and her coach was mad. "I don't want to talk about it," she said.

"That's real great. Here we plan and could have gotten first and second and you don't want to talk about it. Thanks a lot."

"All right, I'll tell you," Doris said, glaring at her coach. "We strategized against you. You were right. If I had gone out with you, I could have had a silver medal for the U.S. He thought you would run a typical American race and wouldn't have anything left at the end, and if I stayed in the pack I could move around the rest of the girls and take the gold medal. But just what you said would happen happened. I got boxed in and had nowhere to go once I made my move. You were long gone and I had to settle for fifth."

I felt bad for both Doris and her coach, and I just walked off. We remained friends, of course, but I'm sure to this day Doris wishes she'd have stuck with our strategy. You're always supposed to listen to your coach, but in trying to steal the gold from a teammate, his greediness had cost her a medal.

Chapter Eleven

JEALOUSY

Being an Olympic champion and a world record holder is an experience so rare that it left me stunned. All I remembered before getting home to Cleveland was that I was besieged by the press for interviews, statements, pictures, and all the rest. It was a heady experience, and I'd be lying if I said I didn't love it.

There was a part of me that hung onto my faith in God. Whenever anyone would discuss religion, God, Christ, the church, or anything connected with faith, I argued for Jesus. But still I wasn't in the Word and my spiritual life was starving to death.

Sure, at the Olympics I had run for the glory of God. I said it and meant it. But I wasn't in fellowship with him. I had become headstrong and independent. I was going to do what I wanted to do, even if I knew it was wrong.

And one of the things that was wrong was John.

I had begun to worry about our relationship because we were so opposite socially. I love to party, to talk, to visit, to make friends. John is a loner.

And jealous? It got to the point where John didn't even want me to talk to my girlfriends, let alone other guys.

He was used to being in the spotlight, and I think he resented my popularity.

When I returned to Cleveland, Mayor Carl Stokes and the City Council held "Madeline Manning Day." I was called the sweetheart, the daughter of Cleveland, and I was showered with praise and gifts. I had asked John to come up from Columbus for the occasion, but I was to regret it.

While I was photographed with the mayor and all the other men, John sulked. I was being hugged and kissed by officials who had known me since I was a child, but even my father didn't like that. Only one photographer asked John to pose with me, and soon John disappeared.

Here was my celebration, my triumphant return to Cleveland. We were at the Top of the Town at Stouffer's for a big to-do, a meal and all. But I couldn't find John. When I got a chance I slipped away and looked for him. There he was in another room, staring out the window. He made it clear that he didn't like all the men hugging and kissing me. I offered to introduce him to everyone. "No," he said, "just go do your thing."

I couldn't take it. How could I enjoy my Day if he was acting this way? "If you want to leave," I said, "let's go. I'm not enjoying this at all."

Somehow we made excuses and begged off. "I'm glad we left," Dad said. "All those men—"

Finally Mother spoke up. She'd had it. I had never heard her holler like this. "This is ridiculous," she screamed, crying. "This is her party and you two have to mess it up! Can't she even enjoy herself once? She has worked for years getting where she is and you harp about somebody kissing her to congratulate her. You should be glad they're treating her like somebody for a change."

John and I had it out later too, but nothing was really resolved. He just didn't want me around those men any more, and I began to fear that he would be impossible to please. From every side I was being warned not to marry him. Both family and friends told me I was becoming sullen, introverted, self-conscious. Down deep I felt the Lord telling me too, but I ignored it. Here was a man I had dreamed about. He was huge and muscular and had his own mind. Sure, it was at my expense sometimes, but I wanted a headstrong man more than a weak one.

And when he suffered a serious back injury playing football that fall, I was really his. I've always been soft when it comes to people who are injured or sick, and my heart went out to him. It's terrible when an athlete has to be set aside from his specialty. As an athlete, I could empathize. He was at a low point, and there was no hope that he could ever play again. His career was down the drain, and I was all he had.

I would be enough, I decided. In a dramatic promise I vowed, "If you can't walk, I'll be your legs. If you can't see, I'll be your eyes. If you can't hear, I'll be your ears. I'll be your hands, or whatever you need." I only wish I would have instead encouraged him to study and plan for an alternative to football as a career. But no, I had even done some of his homework for him. We had both fallen so short of what God wanted for us that the most foolish thing we could have done was to get married.

John became bitter about athletics. The world that had been his life had turned on him and injured him, and now everything was gone. Physically, he could have done anything. Psychologically he was an athlete. Nothing else interested him. He didn't want to see a football game or even hear about any other sports.

In 1969 I was the outstanding athlete in the America vs. Europe Games in Germany, but when I returned it was hard for him to take. I was flourishing. He was suffering. My success made his disappointment more acute, and he was even jealous of my ability. I wanted so badly to prove that I loved him that I decided to marry him to make him happy and to prove my point. I thought it would convince him I was his alone, so he wouldn't have to be jealous. But he always said, "It's not you I don't trust; it's those other people."

We were destined for disaster as husband and wife. I was far from God, reveling in my track success, and interested only in proving something to John. He had nothing, and I thought he needed only me. He had no job, and his bitterness crippled his future. I was depressed by it all, and people noticed.

"What's wrong, Madeline?" my friends asked.

"Nothing," I'd lie, trying to convince myself. "I'm happy."

Meanwhile John's mother had told him, "You don't need a girl like that." *That* meant dark-skinned. John's family were light-skinned blacks, and I was the first dark-skinned girl he had ever been serious about. All the indicators pointed against us, not the least of which was my popularity with the press as a sports heroine. We decided we'd get married and tell only our parents and my coaches. The last thing we needed was press coverage. I don't think John could have handled being Mr. Madeline Manning, and it wouldn't have been fair to him anyway.

We were married in the fall of 1969 when I had three quarters to go to finish my requirements for a bachelor's degree in sociology. Married life was rugged from the beginning, but I want to make clear that I take much of the blame. First of all, I shouldn't have married John, knowing that our personalities were opposites. There's nothing wrong with being introverted and not a people person, but I should have known that I wouldn't function well with someone like that.

And in trying to change him or change for him, I was attempting the impossible. I married a man who had an unhealthy need for my comfort and attention. He was hurt physically and psychologically by not being able to play football, and I was in no spiritual condition to help him.

What I should have done was shower him with love and submission and encouragement, and especially forgiveness. The Bible says that a soft answer will turn away wrath. But when he forbade me to even watch track meets on television because it bothered him to see healthy athletes, I argued. Maybe if I had agreed and catered to him until his bitterness healed, things would have smoothed out. But no, I insisted on watching.

I gave up running in early 1970 when I discovered I was pregnant. That made it doubly hard to have to fight when I wanted to watch my old friends run on television. I liked to watch football too, but that was strictly forbidden. I was born an athlete and competition is part of me. I couldn't stand being restricted from just watching. When Lee Evans or anyone else I had been close to during my running days came on television, I got all excited and cheered while they ran.

"You still like him, don't you?" John would say. "You wish it was him here instead of me."

"That man has another woman," I'd respond, not realizing that was not what John wanted or needed to hear.

When the first quarter ended at Tennessee State, we quit school and headed for Columbus, where we moved in with John's mother. I had just two quarters to go to get my degree in sociology, and the University was nice enough to tell me I could come back and finish up, under scholarship, whenever I was ready.

We had no money and no apartment of our own, and I began bugging John to find us one. "Let me go to Cleveland and live with my mother," I said. "I can find a job there and send you money to get us set up in a place." That worked for awhile, or so I thought. I was pregnant, working full-time, and living with my parents in Cleveland while John was supposedly using the money I sent to get us an apartment. As it turned out, he was spending the money on his car.

After I had Little John in August of 1970, I had to remain in Cleveland for a month until I was strong enough to get out and get a job again. We finally got an apartment in Columbus, but things were so rocky, and John was so upset about the assembly line job he'd gotten, that I could hardly take it. He was working long hours for low pay, and he hated the work.

Little John was just a few months old when John and I talked it out. "I have only a couple of quarters to go," I said. "Why don't I go back to Tennessee State and finish up, and then I'll get a good job and work while you finish school. Then we'll both have degrees and you can get the kind of job you want." Of course, John wouldn't be able to take care of the baby while I was in Nashville, so his mother got the job and John moved back in with her.

It tore me up to leave my baby in April when he was just eight months old, but I knew it was our only hope of eventually holding the family together. I couldn't do anything to please John. He was miserable and spent his time tinkering with his car when he wasn't sleeping, eating, or working. I truly hoped that I could get a good job so he could finish school quickly and get into coaching or whatever he wanted. I figured if he was happy, we'd make it. And he sure wasn't happy.

I still don't know how I stayed away from Little John for a whole quarter of school. My friends and family were against it, of course, and I wouldn't recommend it either. But sometimes you do what you have to do. John didn't make it any easier, though we had already agreed on my going. He claimed he missed me and that he felt it was wrong for me to be away from my baby, but I have always suspected that he missed my weekly income added to the family budget. I cried myself to sleep many nights, longing to cuddle my baby. When John called he would threaten me if I didn't come back. He even threatened to come and get me. He put Little John on the phone and surprised me with the words he was learning already. I would cherish the pictures they sent me, and it was amazing that I made it through the quarter. I had planned to finish the one remaining quarter, but I couldn't stand being away from Little John. The only thing that kept me from going insane without him was that the very reason I was away from him was so that he could have a better life. I would take some of the burden off his daddy, and we would work together to make more money and provide a nice home for our child. If I could just work in two more quarters at Tennessee State, I thought we'd be a giant step ahead. But after that first quarter I couldn't stand it any longer.

It was a thrill to get back and see my baby, though things at home were worse than ever. I thought John wanted me home to take care of the baby so he could work, but soon he was bugging me to get out and get a job. We finally got our own place. Nothing was solved, except that his mother had to spend less time taking care of Little John. We fought about everything.

My only link to God was going to church Sunday mornings and evenings and on Thursday nights for choir practice. My devotional life was still shot, so I have to take much of the blame for our crumbling marriage. I had no alternatives, nothing to offer. We were drowning in selfishness and pettiness and jealousy. And rather than trying to fix things up by seeking God in the situation, I tried fighting fire with fire. When I was right I taunted. When I was wrong, I felt I deserved the right to be wrong once in a while. It seemed we did nothing but argue. Often we fought physically, but of course I was no match for John. Only God, or Little John's screaming, or John's common sense kept him from really hurting me.

He began staying away from home for longer and longer periods. I had tried to get him to go with me to a marriage counselor even before I went back to school, but he had refused. Now he wanted me to go to one, but I found out it was a white girl he had been counseled by while I was gone. She knew the whole story before I could tell my side.

She hassled me for leaving my baby while gallivanting off to college. And she hardly let me explain. John contradicted me and we argued right in front of her. That was when I realized it was hopeless. We were at an impasse.

One day he even tried to forbid me to go to church. He'd been complaining about my going three times a week, and now he didn't want me to go at all. He thought I just wanted to be around the men in the choir (most of whom were twice my age).

Perhaps if I had been submissive and obeyed him, it would have blown his mind and he would have seen how ridiculous the situation was. But I was in no spiritual condition to do that. The main reason I was going to church was to get out of the house once in a while. Of course I liked the fellowship, and often God spoke to me through the services. But still I was not in tune with the Lord.

I tried to tell John that going to church was the way I worshiped the Lord. "I am your lord," he said.

That was it, the end. That I could not accept. If we had been spiritually right, sure he would have been the head of the home, and I would have been responsible to him and he would have been responsible to God for me. But my Lord? No. There was no way he could take the place of my Lord, and I told him so.

As I am sure happens in so many broken marriages, each of us thought the other was the culprit. The Lord has given me peace and allowed me to forgive the things I felt John did wrong to me. And I hope that's true the other way too. Still, when it all tumbled in upon me—the whop trip of realizing that our marriage was hopeless—I just about freaked out.

I had done my washing and was sitting among the clothes, trying to get them folded. It was just Little John and me in our apartment. I sat staring at the wall and suddenly I had no will to move. I felt like doing nothing. I was tuning out the world. The phone rang and rang. I heard it but I didn't hear it. Little John pulled a stack of clothes over and toddled around the place getting into everything. I was devastated.

What had happened to us? I had been raised as a good girl, and I had grown up to be a God-fearing woman. I was a champion athlete, a popular person, a leader at church, a soloist. Everybody liked me and thought I had my thing together. And I did. Except in the most important area of all. My marriage was breaking up, and nothing I did was going to change it. The only thing I can determine now is that I felt powerless. Nothing mattered any more. Did I still love John? Had I ever really loved him? Had I been selfish, unbending? Was I hurt because he was rejecting me? Was I rejecting him?

I really didn't think so. I thought that if he would come to me and try to get things straightened out, I would do anything to make it happen. That's why I couldn't believe he was actually abandoning me. I would see him one day, but not for the next three. And when we saw each other, we only argued. After months and months of heartache, there I sat in my apartment, unable to move. I felt as if I would die if my breathing had to be voluntary.

I was in a daze, probably akin to a drug trip (though I wouldn't know). My life was crumbling around me and I had nothing to draw from. No daily Bible reading. No consistent prayer life. God was there and waiting for me to turn to him, but for many reasons, I couldn't do it. Maybe I didn't believe he would really forgive my inconsistency. Maybe I knew he would search my heart. Anyway, the result of my turmoil? I was a zombie.

Someone was at the door, but still I couldn't move. I

don't know if I even blinked. My arms hung like weights from my shoulders. I was humiliated. Defeated. Had the apartment building burned to the ground, I'm convinced I'd never have moved. To this day I don't know how Little John got the three locks on the door unlatched and let in my girlfriend and her husband, Sol and Waverly Espie.

I didn't even look up. "I knew you were home, but you didn't answer the phone. I was worried—" She could tell I was out of it. I hadn't even looked at her yet. "Madeline," she said evenly, "let's get out of here and go for a drive, huh?" She gathered up Little John and led me by the arm to her car. I was not accepting my defeat. I was retreating from my disaster. God had sent her and Sol. Who knows what might have happened to me in that frame of mind if they hadn't come?

We drove around and around for hours, and Sol just talked the whole time. He was nervous, realizing I was upset. And he was trying to take my mind off whatever it was that was bothering me. But finally he struck too close to home. He was going on about how crazy the television soap operas are. "Some of that's probably true in real life though," he added, laughing.

It sure was. I burst into tears, an encouraging sign to Waverly. I never would have dreamed that my own marriage would break up. Here I had been on top of the world, and I knew exactly why I had toppled off. I had been disobedient to the Word of the Lord. I had been warned from every side that John was a man who would demand more than I could give, that we would never hit it off as man and wife because of our opposite personalities. But more than just my friends and relatives told me. The Lord himself had impressed it deep on my heart, yet I had willfully disobeyed. I was now paying the price. And I was learning a valuable lesson too.

After I cried it out, I left John and moved in with Sol and Waverly. They were runners too, and I found that working out with them after a day at work was one way to release my frustrations. I was still deeply depressed, but I was praying more and working out a lot, and I found myself quickly getting back into shape under the tutelage of Ed White, coach of the Columbus Community Track Team. I had planned to run through 1972 when John and I were first married, but with his injury and all, I felt pressured to quit when I had Little John. I had given up hope of ever running again until John and I separated. Then I began running just to get my mind off my troubles. But under a good coach, and as upset as I was, my workouts were hard and long. My times were getting better and better. It was already late in 1971, and here I was trying to get in shape for the '72 Olympics in Munich.

I should have slowly worked to a peak, but there was no way. I began to sniff that Olympic fragrance, and soon I was chugging away in earnest. I won't say my psyche was much better, but I was running, and once again I had something to look forward to. I had already decided that after the Olympics, maybe in the winter of '73, I would get back to Tennessee State to get that last elusive quarter out of the way. I didn't know what would become of John and me, but I wasn't going to shrivel up waiting for it.

Chapter Twelve

MUNICH

John and I were divorced before the end of 1971, and the Lord took us both through some more trials and testing. I think we were both given an extra measure of love and peace so we wouldn't harbor hatred for each other, and I believe too that we have forgiven each other. Over the next year or so, until he was married again, we talked briefly about the possibility of getting together again for Little John's sake, but nothing ever worked out. That was for the best, I'm sure. Little John is better off with his parents several miles apart, as hard as that is on a child, than with them together and fighting all the time.

Through it all, God brought me to the end of myself, at least for then. There would be times later, and even now, when he had to rope me in and remind that in myself I will fail. It's sad that he has to let us get to the end of ourselves before we'll look to him, but that seems to be the pattern all too often. I used to think the whippings I got from my mother were hard to take. When the Lord chastises you, you know what a whipping is. And he whips me for the same reason my mother whipped me. Love.

It would be after the '72 Olympics that God would really get me on the right path, but for early 1972, he was spiritually building me back up. There was still bitterness. I felt a bit cheated, still somewhat depressed. I had had a real downer of a year and I wanted to reward myself with another gold medal or two at the Olympics in Munich. Had I had any idea what I would go through in Munich, I would have stayed home.

Lee Evans, who had also been married and divorced since the last Olympics, invited me to bring Little John out to California for awhile before the Olympic trials and all the other big meets that would precede it. It was just a friendly gesture, and I took him up on it. It was good for Little John and me to get away and just relax in the sun. And Lee was such a good friend.

We had talked in the past about the possibility of marriage, but that was before I had met John, and now Lee and I were both still smarting from bad marriages. I think we still thought our day might come, but we let it ride while I was visiting. Our wounds were too fresh. I was still bitter, and we agreed to talk about serious things after the Olympics.

The rest and relaxation really paid off for me. I came back East strong and ready, and began winning every meet I entered. In the annual Pioneer Meet in Philadelphia I ran a 2:02 half mile to tie my world record. (2:00.9 was my 800-meter record.) Now I would be a favorite, and it was as if I had never retired or had a baby. But that baby became another bone of contention.

At the Olympic training site in Urbana, Illinois, I learned that the U.S. Olympic committee would not let me take Little John on the charter flight to Munich, and that even if I got him there another way, someone else would have to take care of him. "Then I'm not going," I said, and I meant it.

At a moment's notice, my bitterness and resentment surfaced and I became dogmatic. I had taken too much for too long. No more Mrs. Nice Gal. I thought I was coming back to the normal Madeline Manning, but when such sore spots arose, I realized that I was still not in the Word like I needed to be. Ol' dummy just wouldn't get her act together.

Because I was a bit older than most of the girls, and because I was well-liked and was a returning gold medalist, the other girls seemed to take to me and rally around me. They decided that if I wasn't going to Munich, they weren't either. I quickly realized that my selfishness had gone too far. I told them that my mother had really wanted to take Little John while I was away anyway, because she didn't like the idea that someone else would have to watch him in Munich.

"You're just saying that," they said. They were right, but I stuck to my story. I didn't want to jeopardize their careers after they had worked hard for years. Little John would stay with Mother at her new home in Louisiana, and the rest of the girls and I would go to Munich. But that brief problem was only the beginning.

Even when we arrived in Munich and checked in at the Olympic Village, I found myself upset. This was supposed to be the richest Olympics in history, and I tried my best to psyche myself up to enjoy it. But something was gone. The thrill of winning the big meets a few months ago and coming through at the nationals and the Olympic trials had just faded away as I dwelt on my year of disappointment. The things I thought would bring me around and snap me out of my depression were simply leaving me empty. Again I was being disobedient to God. I knew all the time that I was not giving him enough time. I can't emphasize enough how important daily prayer and Bible reading is. He was impressing it upon me regularly, and I was ignoring him. And I would pay.

Soon after I arrived at the Olympic Village, a group of young people came through witnessing for Christ and asking if anyone wanted to join in a Bible study and prayer time. "Yes, I would," I said quietly. A few other athletes joined us and we had a beautiful quiet time of sharing and prayer. But I didn't see these Christians again during the entire Olympics, and I never knew who they were. Worst of all, the experience didn't push me into a solid devotional life as it should have. A feeling of gloom came over me, and try as I would to encourage the other athletes and stay on top of things, this was not going to be my Olympics.

When I realized that Lee Evans had brought another girl to the Olympics, I said to myself, *Forget it. That's it. No more serious thoughts about guys.* It pointed up to me that I really had harbored a hope of something happening between us some day. I had tried to push it from my mind and I had convinced myself that I was not really ready yet to consider it. But now here he was with another girl, and, believe it or not, she looked a lot like me. She wore her hair the same way I wore mine, and she was tall and thin. Another possibility down the tube, and more reason for me to retreat into a protective shell. I was not the Madeline Manning I had been. I knew it and was powerless to change.

I got tired of just working out and being penned up in my Village room every night, so I started bumming around with a few other girls and guys. We would dance at the discotheques, and while I wasn't into drinking or anything real loose, I was just letting myself go. I wasn't sleeping as much as I should have, and I wasn't acting saved either. In my own selfish way, I felt I was rewarding myself for all I had been through. Self-pity was the name of my game.

Before we 800-meter runners were scheduled to get lane assignments and numbers, we decided to check out the track and talk to the U.S. men sprinters who should have been on the track warming up for their preliminary heats in the 100-meter dash. Eddie Hart and Ronnie Ray Robinson were the two fastest runners in the world and were looking forward to avenging the U.S. loss to Russian Valery Borzov in both the 100 and the 200 in several international meets since the '68 Games.

Cheryl Toussaint and I had noticed that the 100-meter guys were not on the warmup track when we were. Our event was *after* theirs, so we knew they should have been there. We thought maybe they had already gotten onto the stadium track, but when we got inside we saw that they weren't there either. One of the girls' coaches was with us, so we told her she had better tell the men's coaches in the stands that Eddie Hart and Ronnie Ray Robinson were not on the track yet. Their event was just an hour away.

I learned later that she went up into the stands and informed two U.S. coaches who were sitting with Lee Evans. "That's Stan Wright's thing," they said. "Let Stan handle it." They didn't budge! True enough, Stan Wright *was* the sprint coach. But something was wrong, and these coaches should have helped somehow.

When Lee realized that they weren't going to do anything, he ran down the stands and pushed his way through the crowd, out of the stadium and all the way to the Olympic Village looking for Coach Wright or Eddie or Ronnie or anyone who could get them to the track before their event. He didn't find them in time, and Stan Wright, a super black coach, every athlete's friend, took the rap for not having his men at the track on time.

It also just happens that Stan was in line for the head Olympic coaching job for 1976. Of course, he didn't get it. We saw him in tears as we waited to enter the stadium for our trial heat in the 800-meter run. Ronnie and Eddie were there too, hoping against hope that they would be able to run in a later heat if the officials would be lenient. Coach Wright had used an old schedule and even that day had had it confirmed as correct by a German official. But it wasn't. And the officials did not let Eddie or Ronnie run in a later heat. Their dreams and hopes and four years of grueling workouts had gone down the drain. And I'll always say, it didn't have to be. Those coaches could have reached Wright or the runners if they had acted immediately.

Here we were, trying to get ready for our heats, Cheryl and Wendy Knudsen and me, and Wright and Robinson and Hart were in shock. We girls were trying not to cry because we had to keep our minds on our own races, but it was a heartbreaker to see those guys' careers on the line. Eddie's times had been better than Borzov's all year, and Ronnie for sure would have finished second. As it turned out, of course, Borzov had an easy final and won both the 100 and the 200.

As upset as we were, it's a wonder Cheryl and Wendy and I were even able to finish our heats. Cheryl had been doing very well and I thought she was ready to peak and run a terrific Olympics, but she ran the worst race of her life. Her heat was very fast and instead of just hanging back and pacing off of the leaders and finishing among the top four, she tried to run with them and simply ran out of gas. She was so upset she couldn't concentrate on the proper strategy. That didn't make my heat any easier either.

I finished second and qualified for the semifinals, but I was so exhausted it worried me. My heat should have been easy. My times had been better than everyone else's in my heat, yet I was distraught and it taxed my body. I shouldn't have been as exhausted as I was after running a mediocre time to qualify. I tried to tell myself it was the effect of seeing the boys and Stan Wright so upset.

Wendy couldn't handle her heat either and failed to qualify. I was disappointed for both her and Cheryl, and began to wonder what in the world else could go wrong. I didn't have to wait long to find out.

Cheryl's coach, Fred Thompson, and my coach, Ed White and his wife, tried to advise me the next day for the semifinals. "Don't try to run anything spectacular," they said. "Just finish among the top four and qualify. Save your strength and your record run for the finals."

It was good advice, of course, and I was glad to have so much support. I got a good night's sleep and had a solid, light workout. I was thinking right, eating right, psyched up.

When we got out onto the track I remembered that the day before I had been a bit confused about exactly where we finished the race. I had just run through at the end without slowing down much, so it hadn't made much difference where we finished. But today, with tougher competition, I thought I'd better be crystal clear on the finish line. (In international competition there is no finishing string or tape, just a line on the ground.)

There were all kinds of lines on the ground at the Munich track because they had sprints and long-distance races and relays, and all of them started and finished at different places. I asked a German official, "Where do we start and where do we stop?"

He showed me where I was to start and I said, "But where do we end?" He appeared annoyed and I didn't get it straight. When we were taking off our sweat suits I asked another runner, "Exactly where do we end?" She pointed to a line, and the German official saw me looking. He walked back to a line and pointed to it. Now I was set.

The race was fairly uneventful, though there were three girls who were maintaining a pretty stiff pace. Had it been the final, I would have stayed right on their heels, or maybe I would have surprised them by challenging for the lead a time or two before the last stretch. But this was just the semifinal, and the first four of us seemed to have put a decent distance between ourselves and the other semifinalists. I decided not to compete for the lead but to just maintain my position.

Coming around the last curve of the second lap, the first three girls began really picking up the pace. I thought it might help me in the final to have them waste a bit of their energy in the semi, so I let them go, careful to look behind me so no one could steal the fourth qualifying place from me. The only runner half close was an English girl, but I was fast closing on the finish line, so I didn't worry.

With about ten yards to go I heard no one behind me, and the three girls in front of me had crossed the finish line and immediately slowed to a walk. I shut down and coasted in too, but after I crossed the finish line I heard the English girl sprinting. She charged by me and I wondered what she was doing. The first three finishers crossed another line about fifteen feet ahead and glanced back as the English girl raced in. They had beaten her to the second line, but she got to the second line ahead of me by two centimeters.

Fifteen minutes later I was informed that I had stopped at the wrong line and that the English girl had finished fourth. I was disqualified, out of the finals. It was slow getting to me. I was dazed. The defending gold medalist had stopped at the wrong line!

People tried to console me, but I wasn't hearing anything. I just walked out of the stadium to the bus back to the Olympic Village. The English girl said, "I know I can't really beat you. I don't belong in that race tomorrow."

"You did the right thing," I told her. "I would have done the same thing."

It was as if I had died. People looked at me with pity. I felt nothing. There was no reaction beyond disbelief. My charge that the official had told me where to stop had gone unheard. The three leaders had stopped at the wrong place too, but their momentum had carried them past the correct line. There was no more hope. I was out of the competition.

I spent the next several hours by myself in my room until Ed White and his wife and Fred Thompson came by
to take me to dinner. I wasn't hungry, but for some reason
I was incredibly thirsty. They tried to make things easier
on me with light talk and ignoring the subject. But as we
sat in a restaurant, waiting for our food, I quickly
drank three small bottles of ginger ale. And suddenly I
wasn't hearing them again.

The whole last year came back to me. My rocky marriage, my separation, the divorce, not being able to bring
Little John, Ronnie and Eddie missing their heats in the
100, Stan Wright getting the short end of a raw deal,
Cheryl and Wendy failing to qualify. And now this. It
welled up inside me. *I never stop at the finish line!* I told
myself. Someone was talking to me, but I didn't hear. *My
momentum always carries me another twenty-five yards
or so! Why now, why this time, why this race? What a
stupid thing to do! Why me? A world record holder, the
defending gold medal winner.*

I was aware of a ginger ale bottle clenched in my fist
and Mrs. White grabbing my arm to keep me from throwing it. I hadn't been able to let anything out, and now it
came in a rush. I burst into tears, slammed the bottle
down, swept my arm across the cluttered table, and
knocked the bottles and dishes onto the floor. I half ran,
half staggered out and down the stairs to the washroom
with Mrs. White close behind.

She stood outside the washroom, not letting anyone else
in, while I hollered and screamed and cried and beat on
the doors and walls. I was at a low, low point, and all
the frustration that had been building since my separation gushed out of me. After all I had done to get back into
shape, now I was really messed up and wiped out.

When Mrs. White heard the noise subside except my
sobbing, she came in and put her arms around me and
cried with me. "Are you all right now?" she asked. I nodded.

It seemed that all the runners who had already competed for the U.S. had failed in one respect or another. Even the ones who had won medals had not won the gold. We losers got together and roamed around downtown Munich until we found a discotheque that was almost empty, but that was playing all the latest American records. We danced and sat around and tried to comfort each other by each insisting that we had run a dumber race than the other. It was a real downer, but we had a couple of days to go before running our relays, so we let it all hang out. Again, I was not turning to my real source of strength, but I was convinced—after Jim Ryun fell in the 1500-meter race, one of our shot-putters had been cheated out of a silver medal, the boxing officiating had been such a disgrace, and our men's basketball team had been robbed of the gold medal—that nothing more could go wrong with the twentieth Olympiad. I was mistaken.

Two days before my relay, in which I was supposed to run the last leg of the 4 x 400 meters, I pulled a muscle in my leg. I figured my chances for even that race were over, and I was depressed. I figured the cards had really been stacked against me. The trainers and my teammates talked me into holding out hope until they saw what they could do with heat packs and various treatments. As it turned out, I was able to run, but my bad leg had short extension, so I had to shorten my stride with the other leg too. It slowed me down a bit, and I'd like to think we could have won the gold medal if I had been at top strength.

I was switched from the anchor leg to the second position, and I did the best I could with my modified stride. We won a silver medal, which was hardly consolation after such a rough Olympics. It was good to be finished with the running part of it, and I decided that the best thing I could do was enjoy the rest of the Games, take it easy, and enjoy partying.

One morning we got in at about four o'clock and crashed into bed. At seven someone came into the room with a story about Arab guerrillas and machine guns and hostages. I had a good laugh, rolled over, and went back to sleep. Not long later we learned that it was true. And we could see the whole mess from our windows. German police officials and sharpshooters dressed in track uniforms had taken positions looking down onto the Israeli rooms where hostages were being held at gunpoint by Arab terrorists.

I had been wondering what more could go wrong, and now I knew. We stayed glued to the televisions almost around the clock, hardly able to believe we were just a few yards away from the terrorism. It was like a nightmare, unreal. Not here at the Games. Not right here in Munich at the Village. I prayed it would end peacefully and that no one would get hurt. But even that prayer would prove futile. The only thing correct in the whole crazy two weeks would be my premonition of impending doom.

Chapter Thirteen

The PREMONITION

I was flat the whole next day. Cheryl Toussaint and I hung around together for most of the day, just chatting and sitting and strolling. I tried not to think of all the things that had gone wrong, but it was hard. The athletic disappointments and all the political inequities seemed minor in light of the Arab-Israeli drama. It was on everyone's minds and lips.

During the day and early evening we visited the men's wing of the U.S. floor in the Village where there was a huge color television. By sunset the Israeli hostages and the terrorists were supposed to have been moved from the Village to the airport. We kept up via television. Some of the athletic events elsewhere in the city of Munich were interspersed with the coverage of the kidnappings, but I grew tired of the whole thing.

Cheryl and I left the television room and headed for U.S. basketball star Jim Brewer's room, which had been converted into a lounge. No one else was there, of course, because they were all watching television. Cheryl began talking about her race. She felt badly about having done poorly, and she probably wanted a bit of consolation from "big sister." But I wasn't listening. I just sat staring out the window into the black nothingness and didn't say anything.

"Madeline, are you listening to me?" I hardly heard the question, and I ignored it. My mind was far away, and I was conscious only that Cheryl was looking at me with a worried face. "Madeline?"

After several more seconds, I said, very ominously, "Cheryl."

"What?" she demanded quickly.

"Something is wrong," I said, quietly, evenly. It scared her . . . and me too.

"What's wrong, Madeline?" she asked. "Are you all right?" Again I ignored her. "Madeline, what are you talking about?"

I broke into a cold sweat and the words tumbled out. "Cheryl, something is wrong, terribly wrong. Something really awful has happened." I stood and shook as I stared out the window.

"I hope it's not the Arab-Israeli thing," she said.

"It could be, I don't know. It might be something else, but it's terrible." I still have trouble explaining the feeling that was washing over me. It was as if my own life had been threatened and I didn't have any escape. "I just feel it," I told her. "I've never felt this way about anything before in my life."

Cheryl sat me down. "Try to calm yourself," she said, and I could tell I had spooked her.

But I couldn't stay seated. I was still shaking, still sweating. I stood and paced. Then, as quickly as it had come, the feeling left me. I plopped into a chair. "Oh, that was horrible. It was like a nightmare!"

"I just hope nothing happened," Cheryl said. "Wanna go watch some more TV?"

We saw Jim Brewer in the TV room and Cheryl told him what I had experienced. "It's probably just a reaction to all the tension here," he said. "You've been through a lot and you have to come down after a while."

"I hope so," I said. (It's true that Olympic pressure really does strange things to you. Many athletes, regardless of how well or how poorly they have done, break down and sob when they've had time to reflect. Others are high for a couple of days, jabbering and goofing around. Still others are just quiet, as if they are trying to believe what they've been through, or as if they are trying to forever burn into their memories the sights and sounds of the Olympics.)

When the announcement came on television that the Israeli hostages had been released and the Arabs had gotten away safely, Cheryl patted my arm. "See," she said, "there was nothing to worry about."

My mind raced. "I wonder what that was then?" I said. *Little John? Mother? Who? Or what?*

"I don't know. You sure went through a thing, didn't you?"

"I sure did."

No sooner had I spoken than the correction came on television. Interrupting the coverage of one of the events, the announcer said, "There has been a mistake. The Israelis have indeed not been released and neither have the Arabs escaped. The latest reports, and these have been confirmed, are that all the terrorists and their hostages have been killed. German soldiers have been wounded by gunfire—"

They showed the chaos at the airport with armed guards running for cover and shooting and the helicopter being bombed. "Oh, God," I cried.

"That's what you felt, Madeline," Cheryl said.

It was the weirdest thing that has ever happened to me, and I still don't know the significance. Maybe God wanted me to be able to empathize with the hostages. Or maybe the spirit of evil was so prevalent in the city that any Christian would have been sensitive to it. I thought the 1972 Olympics had been bad enough, but the killings and the premonition had put the icing on the cake for me. It was hard to sleep, and though the premonition of disaster never returned, the bad, scary feeling from it remained for a few days.

The whole of Munich seemed to be in mourning, and I felt bad for the people who still had to compete. There was a perfunctory memorial service and the competition continued, against the wishes of many athletes and fans. The Games were delayed one full day, and that caused havoc with chartered plane schedules. Many fans and athletes left a day before the closing ceremonies, and it gave me a chance to reflect on the irony of the richest Olympics in history.

I believe that with the betting that was going on, the politics, the racial prejudice, and the mockery of the witness for Christ of some young people (a Russian athlete tried to seduce a girl who offered him a Bible), God pulled his protection from the whole scene and Satan had his way with terrorism, destruction, and death.

A spirit of gloom settled in, and as brave and cheerful as everyone tried to be, my friends and I were devastated. The athlete who had been more impressive than any other in history, swimmer Mark Spitz, who set seven world records and won seven gold medals, had to be secreted away because he was Jewish. And the funeral service for the slain athletes was another downer.

The whole experience sobered me to a degree I wouldn't have thought possible. I was in a kind of daze. I had known the leveling disappointment of defeat, but that was nothing compared to this hopelessness and despair. Perhaps nothing else could have made me realize that I had no resources for life's biggest problems. But now I knew as never before that only God could make me what he wanted me to be. And nothing else mattered, after all.

Without him, terror reigns. My time of recommitment was yet to come, but the 1972 Munich fiasco at least stopped my outbound journey and pointed me in another direction.

My trip back to total dependence upon God in everyday life would take almost a year, but I learned some more lessons before and during my last quarter at Tennessee State. I had had two offers during the Olympics, one to come and train my voice with Roberta Flack in Seattle (I could hardly believe it), and the other to coach college track in Pomona, California, a beautiful city with a near-perfect climate. Those two opportunities awaited, and I was convinced that I would never have to weather the horrid winters of Cleveland again.

My parents kept Little John in Louisiana at their new home while I finished the last two and a half months of school and finally graduated from Tennessee State with a major in sociology and a minor in history. Then, convinced that I was sold out to whatever God had for me, I prayed that he would direct me to the ministry of his choice—provided it was a choice between Roberta Flack in Seattle, and coaching track in Pomona, California.

I had a lot of track friends in California, so that would have been perfect. I wanted to be a hotshot gospel singer too, and I had been in a state of shock ever since I heard that Roberta Flack had actually heard of me and wanted to help train me musically. So, singing would have been okay too. But I really was seeking the Lord in my future. I prayed that he would show me the way, and though my mind was somewhere on the West Coast, I promised him that I would be open to his leading.

In one day, he set up everything.

My roommate, Diane Hughes from Cleveland, came back from her final exams during that last week at Tennessee State and saw me packing. She knew I had no job lined up, no money even to get to Louisiana to pick up

Little John, no nothin'. "Did you get something?" she asked.

"No," I said, "I've just been seeking the Lord, and he told me to start packing."

She looked at me dubiously. "Oh."

I kept packing, trusting the Lord to do whatever he was going to do. I just wished it would happen soon. I had done nothing for the past two weeks but study, cramming for finals and worrying about every last grade point. It was over, and I was glad about that, but what now? What was I going to do with my education, my hard work, and my degree? Like Bob Hope says, you have to major in something to know what kind of work you're out of!

I was nearly finished packing when someone came by the room and told me I was wanted on the dorm phone. It was quite a scene with girls packing to leave for home and various careers, but I'll bet I was the only one who didn't know where she was headed. It could have been anybody on the phone. But it wasn't. It was somebody.

"Hello?"

"Madeline Manning Jackson?"

"Yes, sir."

"This is Major Henry Gariepy of the Salvation Army Hough Multi-Purpose Center in Cleveland."

"Yes, hi, how are you?" I said, all the time saying to myself, *Oh, no, not Cleveland. I know the Lord doesn't want me in Cleveland, of all places!*

He told me he had been trying to locate me for a month and was glad he had found me because he needed me at the Center. "We had a hundred girls come in to apply, but only two met the requirements. One didn't show up for work, and the other worked for a week before deciding that she couldn't hack it. Then my wife, without knowing that I had been trying to locate you all this time, had a dream that she saw you working here. The job must be for you."

I wasn't quite prepared for him to list everything I always had wanted to do and had studied and trained for. But he did. "There'll be heading up the recreation program in a social service capacity. It will involve some public relations, some spiritual guidance counseling, and whatever else you feel you'd like to initiate, like drama or music."

The money was adequate, perfect in fact, and I was nearly speechless. I asked him if I could call him back later, because I wanted to be sure the Lord was in this. I didn't want to be swayed by my dire need, or by his wife's dream, as valid as it may have been, or even by the fact that it all seemed so perfect. Maybe in the back of my mind I was hoping that I would still be somehow led away from Cleveland to the more tropical climate of the West Coast. But for whatever reason, I postponed my decision.

Later that evening, after I was finished packing, Major Gariepy called again. "What do you think, Madeline?" he asked. "Have you prayed over it and made up your mind?"

"I'll tell you something," I said. "This is really quick, but as you probably knew when you first called, the Lord was speaking to me. He has impressed upon me that this was what he had me packing for. I wasn't ready to accept it because I had decided I wasn't coming back to Cleveland. Now I know it's what I'm supposed to do."

"Can you start tomorrow?"

"No," I laughed. "Give me a couple of weeks to pick up my son and get some business squared away in Columbus."

"Everything else is okay, then? You don't need anything?"

For a split second I was tempted to ask if he could send me my first paycheck in advance, because I was literally down to my last quarter. But the Lord impressed me not to ask. He seemed to be telling me, "I will provide a way."

"No," I told the Major. "I'm all set and I'll see you in

two weeks." I praised the Lord for the new opportunity, but I didn't know how I would get off campus, let alone get to Louisiana and then Columbus and Cleveland.

As I got back to my room I heard the dorm phone ringing again at the other end of the hall. With all the girls in the residence center I knew it couldn't be for me again, but I decided to answer it anyway. Sometimes no one answers it and someone misses an important call. Surprisingly, it was my Aunt Georgia.

She had already heard that I had gotten a job in Cleveland because the Major had called her, looking for me. "I know you have no place to stay here, so when you come, you stay with us." God was really opening doors. Now I knew where I was going, but I still didn't know how I was getting there.

When I got back to my room and closed the door I heard the phone ringing again. This time it just *had* to be for one of the other girls, because with everyone getting ready to go home there could be any number of messages. Someone else answered it, but, sure enough, it was for me. *Now, who could this be?* I asked myself. *Lord, I am not even going to ask you how you're working things out, because you've done it all up until now.*

It was Bob Talley, an assistant coach I had worked under in Columbus. "I heard you were coming here to pick up your car and some of your stuff at the Espies. You and Little John stay with us while you get your business straight here, huh?" What would God do next?

Later that night I was in the lobby on the main floor of the dorm when the receptionist told me I had a message from my coach. He wanted to see me at the post office. I hustled over there, and Mr. Temple asked why I hadn't picked up my mail for several days. "I've been studying too much I guess," I said.

"You've got a pile of mail here," he said.

When I finished opening it all, between congratulations

on my graduation and just love gifts from friends, I stood there with $150. "This is amazing," I said softly. All the phone calls and the money had come within about four hours.

While I was in Louisiana to pick up Little John, I received even more money from friends. And when I got to Columbus, a $50 check from Doris Brown was waiting for me. The Lord had led her to save her tithe and send it to me.

God had so forgivingly prepared the way for me that I began to really seek him. I was into my Bible more every day and anxious to have all that he wanted for me. And that would be a lot by the end of 1973.

Chapter Fourteen

In RETIREMENT - and Out

After the '72 Games I retired again, and this time I really thought I meant it. Even during that last quarter at Tennessee State when I helped Mr. Temple coach the girls, there were times I wished I could take off and get in shape again. But I believed my time was gone.

I wanted to get my degree requirements out of the way, get my son, get back to work, and forget about competing. I did enjoy coaching, though, so when one of the Tigerbelles, Rozella McClure, said she wanted me to coach her in Cleveland during the summer, I agreed. She joined me a few weeks after the quarter ended, and she planned to train under me until school started again in the fall of '73.

At 5-7 and about 140 pounds, she was a big girl, and we nicknamed her Country. She was a hard-working, strong-running girl from Georgia, and we really hit it off together. As it turned out, Rozella never went back to school. We roomed together until January of '76, when she became Rozella "Country" McClure Early. But it was spending time on the track with Rozella that started a yearning deep inside me to get back into running. I fought it and fought it and fought it.

Madeline, age 9, seated beside her brother. Standing, left to right: Madeline's father, mother, sister, and aunt. Two brothers are not shown.

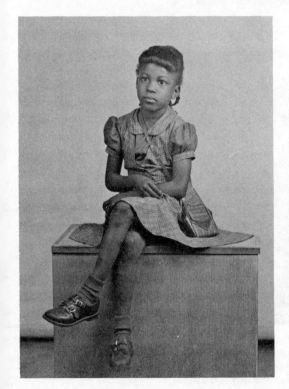

Left: Studio portrait of Madeline, age 8. Below: John Hay High School graduate Madeline Manning in home photograph by her mother.

Madeline breaks tape at
University Games in Tokyo, 1966.

Proud mother and sister greet returning
Olympic Gold Medal winner Madeline
Manning at Cleveland airport, 1968

Winning takes hard work . . .
(Paul Tepley photos)

. . . and getting used to hurting
(Sandy La Corte photo)

Madeline in interview with CBS announcer
Rick Barry at Pan Africa, Germany, U.S. Games
in Durham, North Carolina, July 1975

Below: Madeline interrupts practice time
to sign autograph for enthusiastic fan
(Sandy La Corte photo)

Madeline and Little John. Left: Time out from training in California for '72 Olympic Games. Right: A tender moment (Sandy La Corte photo). Below: Working out (Paul Tepley photo).

Presidential welcome to track and field athletes at Plattsburgh, New York, Olympic training site, June 1976. Left to right: Doris Brown Heritage, Kathy Weston, Madeline, President Ford, Wendy Knudsen, Coach Alex Ferenczy, Cindy Poor, Francie Larrieu Lutz. Below: Relaxation time at training site.

Little John and Madeline's best friend, Wanda Curry (carrying Bible), go with Madeline to speaking engagement at Dover, Ohio, church.

Madeline shares the podium with recording artist Ray Hildebrand at a Pennsylvania meeting of the Fellowship of Christian Athletes. Ray is an FCA staff member and on the National Board.

Salvation Army staffer Madeline Jackson joins girls in prayer and Bible study (Sandy La Corte photos)

"Is that me?" Madeline works with Terry Jamison, manager and producer, at Golden Voice Studios in South Pekin, Illinois, September 1976.

I met Wanda Curry in 1973 too. She's the girl I room with now. Wanda worked in the Hough Center that summer, not sure where she was going to school in the fall. I began witnessing to her and we became friends. She seemed to have good physical flexibility from what I could see when she was goofing around in the gym.

"Do you have any interest in gymnastics?" I asked.

"I like it. I was a cheerleader, but I don't really know much about it."

"Would you be willing to teach gymnastics if we got some books and studied up on it?"

"Sure."

We bought some books and read them, and I tried pulling Wanda in every different direction. I was *really* a dummy about gymnastics, having never gotten involved even in modern dance while running all the time in high school. But I wanted a gymnastics class for young kids, and it seemed like Wanda would be a perfect teacher if I could help her learn the basics. We learned together, but she had better flexibility than I did.

We worked on a dance that helped develop and show off her flexibility, and when she went to Illinois in the fall to attend George Williams College, she used the dance as a tryout for their gymnastics team. All the other girls there were experienced from high school teams, but Wanda made the team and even became a state champion. By the time she returned to Cleveland, she was really the gymnastics expert, and she's doing a great job with the girls.

Wanda has become a beautiful sister in Christ, and we are really close. We've gone through many things together and have grown spiritually to the point that the little things that would bother most roommates are very little problem for us. We work out our schedules so we can help each other, and we just love each other in the Lord. It's not easy for a young girl like Wanda to live with an old-timer like me and a six-year-old rambunctious boy like Little John. But the Lord has made it work out.

Three others that I met in 1973 were very important in my Christian life. Willie and Shirley McKinney, whom I met through the Cleveland chapter of the Fellowship of Christian Athletes, became my spiritual big brother and sister. And Carl Raney, a young minister and musician from Milwaukee, Wisconsin, was also instrumental in answering my thousand and one questions about a closer walk with Christ.

These Christian friends and counselors encouraged me to seek God with all of my heart and life. Carl admonished me to study my Bible hungrily, and he prayed with me nearly every day. Sometimes we would just call each other and share blessings over the phone and pray together. Whatever it was that he and the McKinneys had, I wanted it. What it was was simply sweet, constant communion with Jesus. And it came by dying to self and becoming alive to God. It was nourished by prayer and staying in the Word.

As I read the entire New Testament and prayed that the Holy Spirit would reveal all of its beauty to me, I found myself drawn into a deeper and deeper love relationship with the Savior. My new circle of Christian friends were different from most I had known. They hungered after God with their whole hearts. Their faith was not something used and then put away until next Sunday. It was daily, living, vital. The more they got, the more they wanted, and I found myself developing this spiritual greediness too.

The more I grew to love Jesus and his Word, the more burdened I became for the lost. I prayed that God would equip me with wisdom and a sensitivity that would make me an effective witnessing tool for him. Sure, I had witnessed in the past, but I wanted power, I wanted to see fruit. I wanted to be burdened for the lost the way Jesus was burdened for me, even to the point of death. I hardly knew what I was getting into, but I knew it was right.

I had always been, and still am, skeptical about all the things people claim as spiritual gifts. I know what gifts are taught in the New Testament, and I know which are emphasized as important and which are considered less important. I am wary of certain methods and procedures, and I believe there are specific biblical guidelines that God has set down concerning how his Spirit will move and work. That caution and wariness made God's work in my life even more impressive to me than it might have been. What he did for me was beautiful, biblical, and right. He gave me a new love for himself and for the lost.

For more than a year I found myself immersed in Scripture and enjoying God as much as I had ever enjoyed track. I was singing and testifying, but I didn't know what God had in mind for me. It seemed as if he were preparing me for an important public ministry. If you had tried to tell me that track and field would be the vehicle, I would have said you were crazy. Something that echoed deep in my head was what I thought had been an insignificant conversation with a reporter at the '72 Olympics. "I won't quit running until I have given my best for God," I told him.

"Well," he said, "what if you don't win this one?"

"I'm not planning on losing," I said. "But if I do, I'll just have to go on and win the next." The more I studied and prayed, the more frequently that conversation teased my conscience. But I kept shoving it to the back of my mind. My service for God would be through the Salvation Army and through speaking and singing. Or so I thought.

Late in 1973 Major Gariepy recommended me to the local chapter of the Fellowship of Christian Athletes. I visited a meeting and was voted in as a chapter member. That gave me another outlet for ministry as I became more known in FCA circles and was able to share my testimony at various functions. The next year I went to the first girls' conference in Indiana. (Now the FCA is building a solid national program for women.)

My spiritual pilgrimage led to Los Angeles that year. I had been invited to participate in an outreach to black Christians by Ralph Bell of the Billy Graham team, and I met many vibrant Christians who were excited about what God was doing all over the country. Just hearing them talk convicted me about my own ministry. I could feel myself being drawn to a deeper commitment of my whole life.

While I was being made up to appear on Ralph Bell's television show, a guy came in who looked just like Andraé Crouch, the black gospel singer who had become a real favorite in Christian circles. I had been introduced to his albums a few months before and enjoyed the fact that he wrote his songs based on Scripture. I also liked the fact that his songs were easy for a voice like mine. So many of the black gospel songs take a real strong voice.

"Who was that guy?" I asked the makeup man.

"Andraé Crouch."

When I finally got a chance to meet him, I discovered that he had been aware of me too. We got to talk over dinner, and after I listened to him for awhile, I began spouting off about all my ideas of witnessing and ministry. I was really getting into it when I realized that I had been talking for several minutes. Embarrassed, I hesitated. Andraé smiled. "Well, preach it, sister!" he said.

I'm sure Andraé thought he had another live one on the line when I told him I was a singer. But he eventually became convinced, and he even wrote the theme song for my album a couple of years later.

Andraé and the other Christians on the West Coast were being used of God to really get to me. The crucial blow came during one of my last evenings there when I

was at dinner with Ralph Bell, the one who had invited
me to the West Coast outreach after hearing me speak at
the Philadelphia Fellowship of Christian Athletes track
meet. He chose that evening to pop the most important
question I had ever been asked.

I had decided to sell out to God, to continue to thirst
after him and his Word, and to commit myself to sharing
the gospel. Why, then, did Ralph have to bring up running? The others had talked all week about how the Lord
was using their talents and abilities to serve him. Was I
using mine, Ralph wanted to know.

He knew I had promised the Lord to give him my best
before I quit. And he also knew what an inspiration the
young people were to me and how it excited me to tell
them about track. People had been asking often why I
wasn't running any more. I had always had an answer before. I was still young, but I did have a child to take care
of. And I had to support myself. And anyway, I thought
my ministry would be in singing and speaking. But when
I ran out of excuses and had pledged myself to God's
leading, Ralph asked the question again.

"Madeline, why aren't you running?"

Sure, it was the same question I had been passing off
for weeks, but now I was deeply convicted. My breath was
short. "Why did you ask me that?"

"I really felt led of the Lord," he said.

"Oh, no," I said. Later in my room I had it out with
God. I didn't want to accept it. I loved my running career,
but it meant sacrifice and hard work. And that's just what
the Lord wanted.

It was an emotional session with God. I cried and
prayed for a long time before I agreed to do whatever it
was that he wanted: "Please show me within the next
week if you really want me running again." I had always
said I was running for Jesus before, but that had been the
extent of it. I knew now that if I ran, I would have to

bear fruit. After learning so much more about loving and serving God, I would be running primarily to reach others for Christ. It wouldn't be a spiritual tag on a running career. It would be a running career as a vehicle to share Christ. Country confirmed it.

When I got back to Cleveland I drove her out to the track so she could work out with Alex and the team. I was going to leave and pick her up later, but she said, "Why don't you stay here and help me a bit?" I stayed. It made me sick to be on that track without running. I finally admitted it to Country. "I haven't told anyone else," I said, "but do you know I feel like running?"

"Oh, Madeline," she said quickly, "I've always thought you should, but I didn't feel it was my place to say. You still have so much to offer. When you help the younger girls and inspire the older ones, it seems they just come together as a team. You minister to everyone and have such an impact. If you were running, think of what you could do."

That was it. I was convinced. I sought out Alex and pulled him off to the side. "Alex, I'm going to run again." He shot me a double take; then he grinned wide.

"Madeline," he said, "I don't know how you can do it, and I don't know how well you'll do, but for some reason I'm happy."

"I'll only run if you coach me, Alex. And this is the last time. I'll be running for Jesus and giving it my all to do my best for him."

"We'll see what we can do," he said, getting excited. "I haven't seen you run for two years, but I think next year could be your year. You're older, the strength is there, you seem spiritually secure, and you have less to worry about than you used to."

Alex, though he never claimed to have received Christ, always knew where I was coming from spiritually. And he was right that I was more mature and had less to worry about. I didn't have domestic hassles, except that I would need time now to train, while at the same time working enough to support Little John and me. And I didn't want to give up my ministering opportunities either. It would mean a long commitment right through the '76 Olympics in Montreal, but I was finally prepared to invest the time.

It was scary. I began running cross-country and soon realized that Alex was right. My age had given my body a certain maturity. I was at the perfect age for a middle-distance runner, and I seemed to be snapping quickly into shape. But would the rest of the track world have already passed me up? My international records had been broken, though my American ones still stood. Could I duplicate them, or do better? Or would I not have the discipline to stay with it? I gave it to God for his glory and decided that my responsibility was to train as hard and tough as I knew how and to make it work schedulewise.

The plan was that I would train for a 1975 comeback. It would be grueling, but with the right plan, the right coach, and finally, the right motive, I was excited. The next year would tell me whether I was capable of competing in my third Olympiad.

Chapter Fifteen

RUNNING for JESUS

I could have chosen someone else to coach me for the '76 Olympics, but Alex was the only logical choice. Who else had known me for so long? Who else cared about me so much? Who knew my weaknesses and my potential like Alex? And who would push me to my limit besides Alex? He was the only coach I trusted. I showed up late for practice more than once in 1975, and Alex jumped on me about it.

"I've been witnessing, Alex," I'd counter. "That's what I'm all about, and in fact it's even why I'm running. You know that. I've got to be obedient to God."

"God also gives you common sense," Alex would say. And he was right. He knew I needed strictness and discipline.

After an inconsistent week in practice, I'd come back on the weekend to win all my events in a big meet. Alex would be shocked. "That had to be God," he'd say. "It sure wasn't you!" Then he'd decide that if I could do that well as easily as I had been training, he'd step up the pace and tell me what I was really capable of achieving. I never really felt capable, but as I honored the Lord with my time, he made things work out for me. I began working harder for God and for Alex, and 1975 started looking like my year. I couldn't lose. God was telling me that the '76 Olympics in Montreal were within reach.

I had never seen more people come to Christ through my ministry than I would in 1975. My speaking and singing ministeries would be especially anointed. There would be power and fruit. On an individual basis too, I would see God work. Teammates, tagalongs, even fans sometimes, would ask me why was I running for Jesus and what did he mean to me.

On Friday nights, whenever I was in town, I made it a point to go to the Cleveland Teen Challenge Center where Nick Pirovolos, a converted convict, headed the ministry. I had met Nick the Greek while singing and speaking at a prison when he was still an inmate. What beautiful Christians he and his wife are! After a life of savage gang fights and bouts with the law, Nick is one of the most enthusiastic believers I've ever met.

But Friday nights were seldom my own. As Alex whipped me into shape, I needed competition to find out exactly where I was on the road to Montreal. When I ran a 2:15.6 half mile in the Pittsburgh Classic meet early in January, it was good for a second place. More stir was created by the patch on my back that read "Running For Jesus." Lots of people were curious about my comeback, but it seemed everyone was interested in my patch.

Alex told the *Cleveland Press* that he wasn't trying to bring me back too fast, since this was my first actual competition since the '72 Olympics. "She's not sixteen or eighteen any more," he said. "And she has other things going. She's working and she has a four-year-old son and she's very involved."

Alex also told the paper that he hoped I would run a 2:10 half mile at the upcoming Knights of Columbus meet in mid-February. By summer, his goal for me was to "come very close to her previous top form" of 1967–68. He really wanted me to build toward the Pan-American Games in Mexico City in the fall. The paper also quoted me as saying, "I always prayed to the Lord and asked for help, but I never felt this way before. My feeling is that the Lord has given us talent and that we are to replenish it and give it back. I haven't done it—yet."

There were, however, the Lake Erie AAU indoor championships at Ashland College before the Knights of Columbus competition, and I felt I badly needed to win my event, regardless of my time. It would do wonders for my head if I knew I could run to win. I ran the 880-yard run and the anchor leg on the 4 x 400 meter relay. My 2:17.3 half mile was no barn-burner, but I did finish in first place. The relay was even more encouraging.

I took the baton, trailing Judy McLaughlin of the Ohio Track Club by twenty yards. She sped to a 55.3 anchor leg, but mine was even faster. I made up the distance quickly and nipped her at the tape. I figured that my biggest need was to get my endurance back to help me improve my times in the half mile. The relay proved that my speed and my competitive edge were already there. The track world began to take notice. I think some of the writers and experts had been watching with skepticism, hoping that the old girl wouldn't embarrass herself with slow times or injuries. They still weren't convinced I could get my half-mile and 800-meter times down to where they needed to be, but that anchor leg on the relay proved I was still to be reckoned with.

I was a bit anxious to get back in top form myself, because while people look up to a former Olympian and world record holder, they don't listen to a has-been. I wanted to be a world-class runner again for the glory of God to maintain a more effective platform of witness.

The Knights of Columbus meet was a biggie, drawing the top male and female stars from all over the country.

Cheryl Toussaint won the women's 440-yard run with a 55.6, breaking my meet record of 55.9, which had stood for seven years. World-record-holding high school sprinter Houston McTear was there, along with miler Marty Liquori and distance aces Mark Winzenreid and Byron Dyce.

I faced a stiff challenge from a sixteen-year-old sensation. Robin Campbell had run a few races in 1974 with times near my American records in both the 800 meters and the 880, but she was not yet in top shape for 1975 either. I broke away early and fought off her late challenge to win by a tenth of a second with a 2:13.1. It wasn't the time Alex wanted, but he and I were both relatively pleased. I was happy to have done well in a showcase indoor meet, and I looked forward to the Tennessee State Tigerbelle Development Meet in Nashville.

I think it was a pleasant surprise for Mr. Temple to see me running again. The *Tennessean* newspaper quoted him, "I thought she was finished. I didn't know that she planned to run again. But she still has that same stride, doesn't she?"

I won the mile in just under five minutes as sort of a workout. Then I won the 880-yard run in 2:23 flat, a long way off my national record. "I'll tell you what happened," Mr. Temple told the sportswriters. "She saw that Judy Smith [of the Tigerbelles] was having some difficulty. So Madeline went at Judy's pace to help her along. That's so typical of Madeline. She was always helping her teammates and other people. Always."

I had an opportunity after the meet to tell the sportswriter from the *Tennessean* that "I've committed my running to Jesus Christ. . . . I had never used running as the No. 1 thing in my witnessing for the Lord. But I decided there was no better way to let the world know about the glory of his gospel."

I felt I was stronger than ever and credited my faith

for that. "Since I've committed my running to Jesus Christ, it's easier," I said. "I have run times already this year that I've never run this early before. I keep surprising myself."

Training became more difficult and more intense. I had to stop working full time, and I was fortunate because Ed Bailey, the new head of the Hough Center, was very good to me on that score. I was able to earn enough money to keep running, but getting to all the meets in distant cities was depleting my reserves. The Olympics were just over a year away, though, and Europeans were already putting the 800-meter record in the mid-1:50s. I had to keep working, keep driving, keep giving, keep sacrificing. What kind of a witness would a mediocre runner be?

To make the U.S. team and tour Russia and Czechoslovakia at the expense of the AAU, I would have to finish among the top two at the National Senior Women's Track and Field Championships in White Plains, New York, the end of June. Alex took me with the team to the Midland, Michigan, Invitational in mid-June for a final tune-up.

It was a big, rugged meet for a small town, and I was pushed hard. I anchored the 1600-meter relay team to a second place, won the 440-yard dash, and won the 800 with a 2:09.1, a meet record. I had finally broken the elusive 2:10 barrier, but it would take a lot better time than that to win at the nationals.

It was gratifying at Midland that the press noticed that I spent a lot of time with the younger girls, witnessing to them and encouraging them. One sportswriter even quoted Alex, "By working hard, she can draw more attention to the good of young people and exercise her religion too."

By then Alex had been named head coach of the 1976 U.S. women's Olympic track and field team, so he was getting almost as much coverage in the papers as were his star runners. The *Midland Daily News* explained how he had come to this country from the Hungarian revolt in

1956. He had worked with young people in track in Hungary, and a month and a half after arriving in Cleveland, the local track club called him. "The only words I could speak to my team then were 'okay,' 'yes,' 'no,' and 'run fast.' "

There's nothing like the smell of the nationals. That's right. The smell. There were over a thousand women at White Plains competing for just a few spots on the national team and the right to be considered one of the early favorites for the Olympics the following summer. And with all those girls came the smell of as many liniments and ointments mixed with the fragrance of fresh fruit and honey used for quick, legal pick-me-ups. The wind blew hot and banners blew from all around the stadium.

Alex told the press that the younger girls would be pushing me. There would be no mercy. I didn't know if I had it in me or not, but I figured I'd just run each heat to qualify for the next until I got to the final, and then I would give it everything. I'd have to, even to finish second in the final and make that international touring team. That could be a life- and a budget-saver. I needed the rough European competition. Anyway, it would take all I had just to get a medal in this meet. It seemed that every American was there.

It was something to see—all the girls of different ages, sizes, and shapes. Some had long, flowing hair; some had it piled on top of their heads. Others had ponytails; still others afros or pigtails.

My qualifying heat was easy and I breezed in to advance to one of the two semifinal heats. I still hadn't been tested to my limits. Nor had I yet approached the American record I had set at the Olympics in 1968. Could I? I knew I would have to to win.

Wendy Knudsen won the first semifinal heat with a 2:08.6, but I was more worried about Kathy Weston of

Wills Stevens's Spikettes from Carmichael, California. She had run simply to qualify for the final, and while Wendy Knudsen was capable of better than a 2:08.6, Kathy was probably even more capable. Cheryl had qualified for the final too, so I couldn't count her out.

As it turned out, we all ran well in the final. Wendy, who had won the other semifinal, finished eighth and last with a 2:04.8. Cheryl was third with a 2:03.1, breaking my 1967 meet record of 2:03.6. Kathy Weston was second with a 2:02.9, but I beat her by almost twenty yards and broke my American record by .4 with a 2:00.5!

I knew the Europeans were running even better times than that, but for me it was a sweet victory over my own record, which had stood since 1968 and Mexico City. After retiring twice, suffering personal and domestic and spiritual problems, and having a baby, bettering my record was a gigantic breakthrough. There were those track experts who said, "Only a .4 improvement in seven years is not enough," but there would be time for more improvement before the Olympics. And I would get some good competition in Kiev and Prague. I was named to head the U.S. women's team on the tour and was also named the outstanding athlete at the national meet. It shook me up to win that honor, because it was a decision by the coaches, judges, and competitors. I was surprised, but many told me they had voted for me not because I had run so well but because of what I meant to them as a person. "You're just good to people," one girl said. "You just love and inspire." I share that here only to bring glory to God, because I simply gave myself to him. He was the one who should have gotten any honor for loving or inspiring people.

I was only twenty-seven, but somehow being the oldest on the U.S. team made me feel older than that. Again it hurt to leave Little John home, but otherwise I looked forward to the trip almost as much as I had in years past. We were scheduled for a meet against the Soviet Union in Kiev, July 4–5, and a triangular meet against Poland and Czechoslovakia in Prague, July 7–8. Then we would return to the U.S. for another triangular, this one against Pan Africa and West Germany at Durham, North Carolina, July 18–19.

While we were on our way to Kiev, the July 7 issue of *Sports Illustrated* ran a report on the national finals. It centered on comments by Ed Temple on the quality of the performers at the meet, and though the article didn't mention that I had run under him at Tennessee State, I was mentioned near the end:

"One veteran who showed sure signs of a return to former ability was 27-year-old Madeline Manning Jackson. At the 1968 Olympics in Mexico City, she won the 800-meter gold medal. She married, had a son, Little John, and was a disappointing fifth in the 800 semifinals at Munich. Now divorced, she works for the Salvation Army in Cleveland and began running again last October. 'I've been surprised one race after the other,' she said after breaking her own U.S. record with a 2:00.5 in the AAU. 'This is about the 20th race I've won since I started running last fall. In this race I was boxed in on the first turn and had to go around four people, which slowed my time. I'm looking for something like a 1:55 at Montreal. The more meets I have, the stronger I get. I'll keep on reaching. I make a lot of sacrifices. Everything I do is for the ministry of Christ. It's time for me to give my talent to the Lord again. I've reached thousands of young people with the Gospel, and I've seen that it has done good. In the ghettos I see people struggling for happiness and peace of mind. I see drug addicts and prostitutes, but I know that you can be somebody with the help of God.' "

The Lord seemed to be blessing my witness. It was all I cared about. Another win or two in Russia and Czechoslovakia would be all right too. My work would be cut out for me in Kiev, where I would face 1974's top 800-meter runner in the world, Lilyana Temova of Bulgaria.

Chapter Sixteen

COUNTDOWN to '76

Russia hit me like a musty room with the shades pulled down. The culture was beautiful, but I could feel the gloom, the void. I was depressed by the dismal, dull shadow.

The next day, when we filed into the stadium for the meet, it was raining, further depressing me. Ironically, the Russians planned the meet to start on the fourth of July. The contrast in national spirit was especially stark as I watched the spectators fill the stadium. It was as if they were fixing to take a final exam.

Where was the running, the shoving, the laughing, the pranks you see at stadium events in the U.S.? Even when their national anthem was played, the Russians rose heavily and sang lifelessly. I was glad it was raining so no one could see my tears. I was looking at their hearts through their faces, and I saw no love, no peace, no joy.

The 800-meter wouldn't be run until the next day, so, as captain of the team, I was free just to encourage the other girls. It was difficult. For one thing, the Soviet women had us totally outclassed, winning every event. And, of course, the weather and the gloom haunted me.

We were hopelessly behind in the meet at the end of

that first day, but that wasn't what troubled me as I returned to my hotel room. My heart ached for the peoples of Russia. I prayed as I had never prayed. I asked the Lord to show me a way that I could do his will in that spiritually desolate country. I felt led to pray more specifically.

Carefully deciding that I should pray what I felt only if I could mean it with all my heart, I prayed, "Lord, use me. At any cost, use me."

The next day, just before the race, the officials informed me that we would be running in our own lanes for the first 300 meters, rather than the usual 100 meters. It shocked me. That meant an entirely different race altogether. When middle-distance runners cut to the inside at 100 meters, there is a lot of bumping and jostling for position before the pace slows and the strategy begins. When they run the first 300 meters in their own lanes first, there are fewer runners left in contention for the lead. The first 300 meters are run faster because no one wants to be too far off the pace when the cut-in is made. Admittedly, the fast pace lends itself to good times, but it's also grueling. But nobody was figuring on any records anyway with puddles on the track growing with the steady downpour.

As I expected, the pace was fast and punishing. I splashed through huge puddles, freezing my legs and flinging mud behind me. No one backed off the pace during the first 300 meters, but the cut-in was uneventful. I half expected the pace to slacken a bit, but the first 400 meters were run in a quick 56.8. I was dying, but determined to stay with the leaders. I wondered if they were hurting like I was. I was already into oxygen debt from the tension and the pace.

As we pounded through the last 400 meters, my breath was gone, but I could hear the others struggling too. Lilyana was leading, but I was matching her stride for stride and we were pulling away from the others. I took a two-stride lead on the backstretch with about 200 meters to go, but Lilyana never conceded defeat.

She challenged me for the lead a half dozen times, pushing me to keep driving, forcing me to keep my arms and legs pumping when I was running on instinct alone. Near the finish Lilyana edged closer but I maintained the lead and won, running a 2:00.3 to break my American record again. I've always wondered how I might have done on a dry day with perfect conditions.

As the only American woman to win an event, I was the only logical choice for American athlete of the meet. That meant an interview on national television. Would an interpreter censor my witness? I left it with the Lord. "I'll say what I'm going to say, Lord, and you use it as you will," I prayed. "I'm not going to ask you how you're going to do it." I never ask the Lord how. I just do what he says and marvel at how he works things out.

The announcer asked a question in Russian and an interpreter repeated it in English: "I understand you have come out of retirement to resume your running career. You reportedly do this for some special reason. Would you expound on it?"

I could hardly believe it! I hesitated, fearing that the interpreter would lose something in the translation, but I had no option but to tell my story and let God handle the rest.

"Yes, I would be glad to expound on it." I said. "I am running for Jesus because he opened the door for me to come out of a two-year retirement to help spread his gospel. I believe that he is the Son of God, and that he died for our sin, rose again, and will return. That's why I am here, and that's why I'm running for Jesus."

Later, one of our group who knew Russian said that the interpreter had translated me correctly. After that I was called into a press conference where more than a dozen from the print media asked me about what I believed and whether or not I taught my son the same way. I assured them that I did. I didn't think they'd really print that in their papers, but many were sent to me later, and they did.

I had more good competition at the Czechoslovakia meet at Strahov Stadium in Prague a few days later. It was hot and dry, maybe too hot. We competed against both Czechs and Poles, and both our men's and women's teams won the triangular meet. I ran a 2:01.9 in the 800, pulling away from Josefina Cerchianova of Czechoslovakia and Elizabeta Katolik of Poland, who were second and third with a 2:02.4 and 2:02.7 respectively. I came back later with a good leg in the 4 x 400 meter relay and was again named outstanding athlete of the meet. That opened more doors with the media for me to share my faith.

Returning to America for the big U.S.–Pan Africa–West Germany triangular meet at Durham, North Carolina, I reflected on the fact that athletically I was doing better than all right. That might sound strange, but honestly, I was so involved in using my new platform for witnessing that—while I was, of course, aware of my times and places and level of competition—I hadn't really let it sink in that I was again becoming the best woman 800-meter runner in the world. It was a good feeling, but I prayed that I would keep it all in perspective and remain consistently conscious that it was a gift of God and had a specific purpose.

The Durham meet was another biggie with all the top men and women runners involved; Rick Wolhuter of the U.S., then the world record-holder in the men's 800, was favored in his event. (Men run the distance about ten full seconds faster than women.)

A crowd of over 10,000 was disappointing to Durham of-

ficials, who had seen bigger crowds in previous years. But
the fans made a lot of noise and added to the atmosphere
of an important international event. And they were
treated to some good track and field.

The men's mile relay team was made up of four black
guys, all Christians. The women's relay team, for the first
time all black, including me, told the guys, "If you break
the world's record, we will too." It was a thrill for me to
see those guys, some babes in Christ but all really saved,
joyful in Jesus. More of the U.S. team was coming to Christ
all the time, and we really began to get close.

It was doubtful that the men could break the world's
record, though they were all in shape, because Fred Newhouse, the usual lead-off man and an Olympian, pulled a
muscle in the open 400 meters on the first day of the competition. With the permission of meet officials, the U.S.
recruited Ronnie Ray, a local collegian from North Carolina Central.

Ronnie hardly ran like a sub. He ran his quarter-mile leg
in under 47 seconds and Robert Taylor kept the U.S. close
with an even faster second leg, though the West Germans
led. Maurice Peoples took the lead for the U.S. on the
third leg and Stan Vinson, my spiritual buddy, ran a
44.9 last quarter for a world record 3:02.4, breaking the
old record of 3:02.8 set by Trinidad-Tobago. Then the
guys jubilantly toured the track in a victory lap, raising
their index fingers. The crowd thought it signified "We're
number one," but I knew different. It was their "One Way
—Jesus" sign.

In the 800 meters I was pleased with a 2:01.5, though
I thought I was capable of breaking two minutes. The
early pace was too slow to allow me to become the first
American woman to break two minutes.

Robin Campbell, Cheryl, Debra Sapenter and I now
had to keep our part of the world-record bargain. It wasn't
going to be easy, because I was coming down with a bad

case of the flu. My body ached and I was tired all the time. I could really feel it coming. I had run the 800, and with about an hour before the relay, cooled down and then had to warm up again. That is hard and not that good for you even when you're healthy. It took a lot out of me.

I ran the third leg and found myself trailing by fifteen yards when I got the baton. I made up five yards quickly, but I couldn't seem to get it on. I stayed about ten yards behind the leader for several hundred yards. At about the 300-meter mark she began to pull away from me, and I didn't have the strength to counter. As I moved into the curve, she was already in the middle of the straight and seemed almost ready to pass the stick to her anchorwoman. I was exhausted but kept pushing. I could do nothing, but I didn't want to embarrass myself and the team by failing miserably and keeping us from even really competing.

The four guys from the men's relay team were shouting encouragement to me from the infield, but it wasn't doing any good. I wished I could just maintain my pace or float or do anything. I felt as if I were in a bad dream, being chased but hardly able to move, let alone run. The only difference was, I was doing the chasing.

Then, instead of the usual "Hang in there!" or "You can do it!," I heard Stan Vinson shout, "Do it for Jesus!" A bunch of little black boys, sitting in the stands directly across from where Stan and the other relay guys were, heard him and picked up on it. They began chanting, "Do it for Jesus, do it for Jesus, do it for Jesus!" Hearing the name of Jesus did something for me. The Lord gave me a surge of strength and I turned on power I didn't know I had. I caught that West German girl quickly and we passed the batons to our anchor runners at the same time. The U.S. girl got a fast start and took an early lead but she ran out of gas at the end and lost by .6 of a second. The West Germans' 3:20.3 was a new world record, as was our 3:20.9, but we had to settle for just a new American record.

The flu hit me hard, and I was laid up for a few days. I couldn't afford too much time away from running so I saw a doctor. He told me that I could run but that I should be the judge because I had a fever and an ear infection. I decided to go to the Baldwin-Wallace track in Cleveland July 23 for the American-African meet since it was so close to home. If I didn't feel well, I could just leave.

I tried warming up but was really wiped out. I bundled up in my sweats and sat in the stands before the meet just to watch for a while, leaning back and supporting my aching body on the seat behind me. I felt like just checking out. One of the girls called to me from the infield and pointed across to the other side of the track. I looked and there was my Salvation Army boss, Ed Bailey, with Wanda and my Sweet Pride gymnastics team of little girls I'd been working with and ministering to for so long. Many of them had come to Jesus through our contact and it buoyed me up to see all those little black hands waving excitedly at me from across the stadium. They held up a banner that read, "Welcome home winner—our winner Mrs. Jackson."

I made my way down and across the field and they just mobbed me, jumping all over and kissing and hugging me. I said, "What in the world is going on?" I hadn't seen them for a long time, and they're like family.

When things settled a little, Wanda said, "I hear you're not feeling too well."

"No, but I'm going to run because I want them to see what Jesus can do. We tell them all the time that he gives us strength. Are we just talking, or does he?"

"Mad, don't go hurting yourself."

"It's the last outdoor meet of the year for me [I had already realized that I couldn't afford to go to the Pan-

American Games] and if I can get through it, I'll just rest a while."

"We'll be praying for you," Ed Bailey said.

Later I learned that a Jewish man in the stands asked Mr. Bailey, "Who is that woman?"

"That's Madeline Manning Jackson."

"Oh, yes, I've read and heard a lot about her. She's really famous and the kids sure like her. They seem to love her."

When I got to the line to run, the girls all bowed their heads to pray for me. The man said to Ed, "This girl must be tremendous if she can quiet this group that was just hollering and carrying on a minute ago. She must be some kind of lady."

When I came past them on the first lap of the 880 I was in the lead, and they were screaming and hollering again. The second time around, battling Kathy Weston and Debbie Vetter, two topnotch half-milers, I was still leading but was tiring fast and in pain. Wanda could tell. She began shouting, "Do it for Jesus! Run for Jesus!" And of course the girls did the same.

I ran a 2:04.9 and beat Kathy by less than a second, with Debbie third, and then I was ready to die. It was hibernation time until the indoor season.

Chapter Seventeen

MRS. JACKSON Goes to WASHINGTON

What a difference between the 1975 season and 1971, another pre-Olympic year. I had been down, disappointed, dejected, away from the Lord. I had been running without purpose and was filled with bitterness. In 1975, with all my hassles behind me and a totally new perspective and goal, I was a free spirit. In Christ, we are free indeed.

Madeline Manning Jackson was so happy and joyful that it must have been hard for some people to believe. I had always been a people person, but now I really had something to say, something to offer. I cared about people and loved them, and it was only because God was doing it through me.

He had loved me and forgiven me and had given me 1975 as a year of promise. I had cut my working time in half, and thus my income was curtailed. Yet he allowed me to get enough money to get to all the meets except the Pan-American Games. And I had been successful. I had beaten the toughest competition in the world head-to-head.

It was a year of his showing me what he could do for me and what he would allow me to do for him.

A knee injury during practice kept me out of the indoor season and I missed the women's AAU indoor nationals. It was hard to train gingerly and try to stay in shape while not having any real competition.

On New Year's Day I was ministering with Nick Pirovolos at Crystal Springs in Ohio when I was convicted about the coming Olympic year. With all that God had shown during 1975, surely one of the most successful years any track athlete had ever had, I knew he had big things in store for me. I had come out of retirement to run for Jesus, and the Olympics and doing my best for God had been the goals. The result was to be an effective ministry for him at any cost, and now I was ready to rededicate myself, and for the first time, dedicate the new year to him.

"Lord," I prayed, "send me anywhere you will, have me do whatever you want. I am fully yours. If there is any weight that might beset me, just move it out of the way."

The Lord had given me so much, especially my apartment on the twenty-fourth floor of a beautiful building. It's more than a flat. It's a home. It's warm. We've had so much prayer there, so much praising and preaching and singing. The whole atmosphere is precious, and when I come home and open the door, it's as if the place welcomes me with a "Hi, Madeline, glad you're here." I can look out from my window and see the sunrise and the beauty of God's nature and his plan for the earth.

I felt particularly blessed in Crystal Springs that New Year's Day, 1976, and during the ensuing weeks, as I trained carefully, I could feel building within me a sense of purpose and destiny for the whole year. God was going to do great things and I was going to be part of it.

For some reason, in my daily Bible reading and prayer the Lord was laying something heavy on my heart. It was a bit unusual and it led me to believe that I might have graduated in a sense in my spiritual walk. My previous months of Bible study and meditation and prayer had been high experiences, happy times. I had been joyous and thrilled and had been pushed into new witnessing opportunities. God had ministered to me that way.

Now he was trying to tell me something. I found myself in the Book of Jeremiah, where God sent the weeping prophet before kings and nations and tribes to proclaim the word of the Lord. The book showed that when a nation didn't listen to the words of the Lord, God sent pestilence and famine and war and the peoples were captured and bound. It frightened me because it was more than just history. It was being burned into me and I had no release for it. Who was I to tell? What was I being taught?

God was taking me from the position of a lifelong Christian who had only recently seen the importance of daily Bible study to a person he had a heavy message for. Don't get me wrong. I'm not talking about a new revelation or a vision. I simply knew that he had led me to study Jeremiah and that he wanted me to apply it some way.

The Book of Jeremiah tells how the prophet warned the people of the judgment of God if they were disobedient. Why would they want to be hassled when all they had to do was obey God? The Lord sent Jeremiah to watch the potter with the clay as a lesson that God would have to break the people before he could mold them into what he wanted.

"God," I cried, "why are you showing me this? I am broken; do what you will with me. Who is this message for?"

I couldn't figure it out, but it laid heavily upon my mind. I switched to the New Testament and read in Third John how a person's life will prosper as his soul prospers. And John wrote something about hearing "that your testimony is still good, you are still faithful" [my paraphrase]. I felt that God was confirming that he was pleased that I was being obedient to him, but it only added

to my wonderment. The message from Jeremiah was one I
was to share. But with whom?

The phone rang. It was Ed Baxter, a friend of Billy Zeo-
li (head of Gospel Films, a sports chaplain, and a friend of
President Ford), calling from Florida. "The President is inviting you to Washington for a professional athletes' prayer brunch. Would you mind coming?"

"Would I *mind*?" There was no response. I was shocked.
"I'm not a professional, you know. I'm an amateur."

"Yes, but you've come highly recommended and we
want you to give your testimony."

"You mean at the White House with the President there
and everything?"

"That's right."

I could hardly respond before the Lord again burned
into my mind the verses he had given me during the last
few weeks. I agreed to come, and I had just a week to
prepare for my two-minute presentation as one of eight
speakers.

It seemed all I could do was fast and pray. The Lord
put the burden of the American people on my heart so
heavily that I was convinced he was about to mete out
judgment upon the nation because we had not spread his
gospel. God impressed upon me that his people had not
upheld their part of the promise in Acts in which he says
we will receive power after the Holy Ghost is come upon
us and we will be witnesses here and to the uttermost
parts of the earth. It was as if he were saying, "My people
have been slack. In this Olympic year I want you and
the other athletes to testify for me unashamedly."

I asked the elders at my church to pray with me, and I
wept. I begged the Lord to have mercy and to see us with
his grace rather than his wrath. For some reason, he convinced me he meant business on this, and I was sure he was
displeased with his people.

No one but the elders and a few close friends knew

what I was going through. It was a rough week of fear and heavy emotion and prayer. I should have been higher than a kite, thinking about meeting the President and all, but I was too upset. This wasn't a joy ride. I didn't know how it would manifest itself, whether I was to speak a word of warning or of love, but I would be ready and open for his use.

I arrived in Washington the night before the brunch and the athletes met for dinner at the Statler Hilton Hotel. Eddie Baxter asked if anyone wanted to share, and the Lord reminded me of his admonition in the Old Testament, "What I give to you, do not diminish a word." I shared that with the others and added that I felt that "the Lord called us here for a specific purpose. We're not only here to rededicate ourselves as athletes to God, but to call America back to true dependence upon God. Although we'll all be under time limits, we ought not to diminish what God wants us to say. The Holy Spirit is intelligent enough to communicate all he has to say through us in a short span."

We prayed and pleaded the blood of Jesus over the entire program. We asked God to give us the spirit of salvation and peace and boldness for his Word. We knew he could touch hearts and change lives.

We prayed three or four different times at as many different places on our way into the brunch at the White House the next day. By the time we were ready to meet the President, the spirit among us was so sweet, you could just feel the peace of God abiding in that place.

As we passed through the reception line, and I kept trying to remember all the protocol involved in meeting the President of the United States, Mr. Ford surprised me by taking my hand and saying, "It's nice to see you, Madeline. How are you going to do in the 800 this year?"

"Pretty good, I hope," I managed. Of course, there was no time for chatting and we moved into a dining room for the brunch.

Rik Masengale, the golfer, was at our table with his wife and several other couples, but there were two empty chairs. I teased Rik. "It'd be funny if the President and his wife sat here with us, wouldn't it? We'd be big shots." Everyone laughed.

After the President entered and made a few welcoming remarks, he left the podium and sat right at our table! "Are you actually gonna sit here and eat?" I asked him, dropping my napkin.

"Do you mind?" he asked, laughing.

"No, I don't mind at all." But I didn't taste much of what I ate.

We had a pleasant chat about the chances of our Olympic teams and I found him surprisingly knowledgeable about most phases.

Once the first of the eight speakers began, it was obvious that the Lord was pouring out his Spirit on everyone. I was thrilled by the short testimonies and I'm sure the President was too. He seemed interested, and was very still.

I was second to last (Norm Evans, the football player, had five minutes to summarize after me). During my two minutes I shared quickly my experience in Kiev and how I had spoken for the Lord over the Russian national television network. "Their god was their government," I said. "But they heard of a different God that day." I also told of my conversion as a child and concluded, " 'As for me and my house,' I'm glad to say, 'we will serve the Lord.' "

Norm Evans ended his five-minute wrap-up in much the same way: "If Jesus is the answer for the whole world today, then what are you going to do about him? I have to say, as Madeline has said, 'As for me and my house . . .' "

The President was very moved by the presentations, and his closing remarks were as spontaneous and inspired as I had ever heard him. He began formally, thanking us again for being there and so forth, but then he pushed aside his notes and looked at us directly as he spoke for several minutes. He affirmed his personal belief in Christ as his Savior and then quoted a lot of Scripture from the part of the New Testament where Paul talks about running the race that is set before us and finishing our course.

Then Dave Boyer sang "America the Beautiful." I never realized how thrilling that song could be. Dave loves it too and really belts it out when he gets to "America! America! [oh, thank God, America]/God shed his grace on thee,/And crown thy good with brotherhood,/From sea to shining sea." He just kept singing and singing, repeating the chorus. Everyone was choked up, including the President. It was during the song that I realized that God had passed judgment upon us that very day and that he had decided to extend the boundaries of his grace to give us another chance in 1976. The prayers of the righteous had come through, and God was again shedding his grace on us. People were just bawling.

There was no denying it now. We were on borrowed time. I didn't know about anyone else, but I would not waver now in my quest to share Jesus at every opportunity. God could have so easily pulled his blessing from this country, and any number of things could have happened to the Christian church. My mission was established, and now I had even more impetus. I wanted badly to die completely to self and be worthy of the calling. God had given us a second chance, and we were to spread his gospel all over the world through international competition.

We had heard that the President could be very formal, but when the brunch and speaking and singing were over, he didn't leave. He unbuttoned his coat, sat back in his chair, thrust his hands into his pockets and just enjoyed talking and laughing. We milled about, getting and signing autographs. I had a nice visit with Mrs. Ford and assured her that many, many people were praying for her and the President.

We were getting ready to see some of the other rooms in the White House when the President asked if he could have his picture taken with me. That was a switch. I had been afraid even to suggest it. We posed quickly and then he put his arm around my shoulder. "I really appreciated your talk," he said. "It inspired me."

"You know, Mr. President," I said, "the Lord has been dealing with me about the judgment he was about to bring on the American people. It made me feel good to know that the man who is over the country I was born in loves the Lord and is able to expound upon his Word."

"Oh, yes," he said, "I love the Lord."

"You just don't know—like I told your wife—how many, many people are praying for you." He nodded, but the Spirit urged me to tell him I loved him. "Mr. President," I said, with every ounce of meaning that surged through me, "I love you. I'm praying for you too."

Tears filled his eyes and he whispered, "Thank you. You just don't know what that means to me."

I didn't think about it until later, but I suppose it's rare for a President to have one of his people tell him that he loves him. And in this case, I'm sure he knew I meant it. It was a message direct from God who was, through me, saying, "Gerald, I love you and I'm with you."

Later, when we athletes were touring the Lincoln Room and some other quarters, one of the White House guards told me, "I've been here two years and I've never been able to come up here. This whole day has been peculiar. None of us has ever seen him like this. So many things are happening and he seems so relaxed."

He was being loved.

Chapter Eighteen

ALL EYES on MONTREAL

As the outdoor season approached and my knee began to repair sufficiently, Alex stepped up the workout schedule, and my lifestyle changed dramatically. I was already cutting down on work time at the Hough Center, but with Little John in school, that meant rising at six every morning to get him ready and off to school.

There were bills to pay, errands to run, a house to keep, meals to fix, my health to watch, ministering to do, a voice to keep in shape, press interviews to do, an album to be recorded, and last, but hardly least, training.

Often I tried to look pained when Alex interrupted a brief breather to tell me it was time for another 60-second quarter. But then he would remind me, "Think of what the Germans and the Russians have been running. It's a matter of training, Madeline. You need no strategy if you are not in shape. Strategy begins here."

He was so right. The best strategy in the world will do nothing for you in the 800 if you are not still among the leaders with 60 meters to go. And the only way to be there is to punish yourself and build yourself to the point where pain and agony is secondary to the goal of being the best middle-distance runner in the world. I felt stronger in every area of my life except the practical. I was spiritually stronger, physically stronger, mentally stronger. It was time I had too little of. Then I would remember the Europeans. They weren't waiting for me. Some were training eight hours a day. If they weren't running they were thinking running, studying running, or dreaming running. They had little else to do, most of them. Some were even subsidized.

I never dwelt on the unfairness of the system and never used it as an excuse. I never had to. Alex and I had all kinds of strategic races we could run as necessary, but we both knew: I had to be in shape.

"Get me back out there," I'd say. "I need three times as much work." And he gave it to me. It paid off.

Olympic fever had hit me like a bad cold, and I wasn't about to let anything get in my way of the gold. Sure the Europeans had reset some of my world records into the mid-1:50s. That didn't deter me. I figured the only reason my times weren't that low was because they hadn't had to be to win. Running near two minutes flat had won any race I was in in 1975, but I knew I would have to shave some seconds off my best time to win at Montreal. And from the beginning, that was my goal. Runningwise, that is. My overall goal was to run for Jesus. But in my mind, there was only one way to do that: as the best, the champion, the gold medalist, the world record holder.

Any athlete has to have that mentality. It would have made no sense for me to come out of retirement for any reason and say, "I'm aiming just to qualify for the Olympics. If I win, that's okay too." No, everyone who seeks a chance at the Games is going for one thing. The top prize. There's no other reason for training. Some have to be more realistic than others and realize that their time is the tenth or twelfth best in the world, so a gold for them would be an upset. But still they have to think it's a possibility.

For me, it was more than a possibility. I had done it

before and I was better than ever. I was running for Jesus so I had my head on straight there. This was going to be my year, and everything in 1975 had pointed to it. Bring on those new world record holders. I was ready for them.

During a prison ministry outreach in Ocala, Florida, in April, I left for Winter Park for my first meet of the year. I was to run the metric mile (1500 meters) as a tuneup, just to see where I was after the knee injury. I ran a 4:29 flat and finished second to Robin Campbell. I was encouraged, as was Alex. We were certain I was ready for a full schedule of meets, and I ran nearly every week from then until the national AAU finals in June.

In a big meet in Trinidad the following week, I ran a 4:34.5 in the 1500 and finished first despite falling during the first lap, rolling over twice, and helping another girl up. Margin of victory? One hundred and fifty yards. In the 800 during the same meet I ran a 2:09 flat and was second to Robin Campbell. I was ahead of 1975, breaking 2:10 much earlier in the season.

A week later I finished second to Wendy Knudsen in the 800 with a 2:04 flat at the Kansas Relays. On April 24, at the Drake Relays in Des Moines, I ran a 4:31.8 1500 in the rain while sick with a cold.

Then it was time to give up the 1500 meters and concentrate on my specialty. Alex still wanted me to run a leg in the 1600-meter relay at the Olympics, of course, but he had given up on my running both the 800 and the 1500. I would rather have run the 400 and the 800, but we finally settled on gunning for the 800 and the relay in Montreal.

My time began really coming down early in May when I won the 800 at the Tom Black Classic in Nashville with a 2:03 flat. Two weeks later, however, I realized that my spot on the Olympic team was hardly assured when I ran a 2:05 at the Modesto (California) Track Meet and finished third to Cindy Poor and Wendy Knudsen. Both looked very strong, and Cindy was also a tough miler. I'd see more of her before the year was out.

My quest for a third Olympic Games was becoming the story of the track world and I was featured in several national magazines. The excitement was building, and I just knew Alex and I were on our way. I worked as hard as I could, and God continued to bless my witness all over the world. In late May I ran two 800s on a Czechoslovakian tour and finished first at Bratislava with a 2:02 (at the world all-comers meet) and first at Ostrava with a 2:00.71, just a blink off my national record.

I got back to the States in time to make the national AAU women's outdoor track and field championships at the University of California at Los Angeles. In three days of competition, with heats, semis, and finals, I ran two mediocre times just to qualify, then came back with a 2:01 to reestablish myself as the premier American woman in the 800. We were a week away from the Olympic Trials in Eugene, Oregon, so there was no more time for speculation as to whether the younger girls were going to keep me from Montreal. I felt good about the time and the competition, and I know Alex did too.

It had been terribly windy at the UCLA track, and I think I could have broken two minutes on a good day.

My chance finally came at Eugene. By then I was reveling in my success at UCLA, having won by a huge margin, and decided not to worry about the other competitors. I was going to go out and take the lead and run the best time I could. It would be the result flashed around the world, and it would be just fine for the European girls to hear that I had broken two minutes in the Olympic trials.

The first heat was so slow that I had no trouble qualifying for the semis with an average time. The problem was that my semi was loaded with talent and I had to run a 2:02 to get into the finals.

Before the final, a TV commentator reminded me that

no American woman had ever broken two minutes in the 800 before and asked if I thought I was ready to do it. "Based on my times in Czechoslovakia and Los Angeles, yes, I think I could possibly do it today."

On the air, it came out this way, "Madeline Manning Jackson said before this race that while no American woman has ever broken two minutes in the 800, after today there will be one."

Oh, well. Luckily, it was correct, though exaggerated. I sped to a 1:59.8, taking the lead immediately and outlasting Cindy Poor who was a close second. The year had sped by as quickly as that 800 meters, and just a little more than two weeks later we were on our way to Plattsburg, New York, the training and processing site for the U.S. Olympic team.

At Plattsburg, Sheila Ingraham, quarter-miler, nominated me for captain of the women's team, and I was elected. On the Olympic team, this means more than just being a big sister or a pep talker. There are a lot of responsibilities aside from helping the others and being a leader, and I enjoyed it.

Sheila and I had grown closer after talking and running with and against each other at several meets. She and I had run together on relay teams too. Many times I had shared with her what the Lord meant to me.

Frankly, however, I'm not always in the mood to share. I don't know if anyone is, or if we are expected to be. That's why I wasn't quite ready for the blond, 35-year-old U.S. kayak racer who approached me in the cafeteria while I was eating with Alex. He tapped me on the shoulder.

"Hi, I'm Mike Johnson," he announced. I hesitated, wondering *who's Mike Johnson?* I figured he was either an athlete or a reporter. "You're Madeline Manning Jackson, are you not?"

"Yes."

"I'm a Christian!"

I think he expected me to say, "Oh, wow, a Christian!" or something like that. All I could muster was, "Oh, that's nice. Praise the Lord for that."

"Yeah!"

I couldn't figure the guy out. He was so zealous that it turned me off. I had been training hard, and I guess I just didn't want to be bothered.

"Do you mind if I sit with you when I get my food?"

I said, "No, go right ahead."

He left to get in line, and I looked warily at Alex.

"He sure is excited, isn't he?" Alex said.

"Yeah," I said. "Maybe he's a new Christian and is just excited about finding another Christian up here."

When Mike returned he monopolized the conversation, telling me about his church and his plans for a ministry at the Games. He was going to distribute Bibles in all languages for Iron Curtain athletes and others. And he wanted to have a Bible study and prayer group right here in Plattsburg, and, and—

I couldn't get a word in edgewise.

"Do you think we could get a group going?" he asked.

"I don't know everyone here yet, but I know they're all busy and I'd hate to impose upon their time. Even the Christians here have to put their training first because it's what God has called them to do. It's their top priority to be in their best shape for the Games."

He agreed, but each time I saw him after that he would assure me that he'd met a few more Christians and that they were all ready. I got the impression that he was telling them the same thing about me. It frustrated me because I noticed that he didn't listen to me and his mind wandered from one subject to the next so that he was hard to follow. If others had the same impression, then he wasn't ministering.

The Lord led me to pray for him specifically about listening and concentrating and being warm and loving to people. Finally I got the chance to talk to him about it. "Mike, can I ask you a couple of questions?"

"Sure."

"First, do you have trouble reading the Word of God? I mean, do you have a short attention span and have trouble concentrating on a message long enough for it to sink in?"

"You know, Madeline," he said, "I'm really having trouble with that. It just seems like, I don't know—"

"Second, about the people you're running into—do they find you a warm and loving person they can come back to just to talk?"

"No. In fact, they really turn off to me, and talk about me and stuff like that—but the Lord told me—"

"Okay, when you do talk to someone else, say a non-Christian, about why he doesn't believe, do you listen?"

"I do, but while I'm talking I might think of something else or see someone else, and it's a problem, yes."

I told him I had been praying for him because the Lord had pointed these things out to me. "These things are important to the spiritual health of you and others. You're zealous and that's great. God will use that, but you've got some pruning to do." We talked for several hours and shared Scripture with each other, and it was good for both of us. It brought us closer for Montreal.

We left for the Olympic Village in Montreal on July 14. That building was beautiful and had some nice features, but when you cram the whole U.S. team on one floor, guys in one wing and women in the other, it's more jammed than pretty. There were eleven girls in my place, which was a single apartment, with one bathroom. That's right. One bathroom for eleven women.

Everyone was kinda excited to get into some competition, knowing that the real stuff was a few days away, so the first evening, Monday, July 14, runners were invited from every team for a twilight meet. I entered the

1000-meter run against six other Americans and an Australian and wound up running a 2:37.5 for first place and a new American record. Admittedly, the 1000 isn't run as often as the more conventional distances, but still it was nice to break the record.

That Wednesday they called another twilight meet, and I ran a 1600-meter relay with Rosalyn Bryant, Debbie Sapenter, and Pam Giles. My 51.8 was the second best on our team that night, so I felt tuned up.

I trained twice a day during the next several days and tried to get my rest while the Olympic Village was hopping. The girls in my room were good. We all covered for each other and answered the phone which was quieted under a pillow so people could sleep if they wanted. I enjoyed looking down into a courtyard from our porch and seeing literally hundreds and hundreds of different country colors. The warm-up suits were just beautiful, and the athletes loved to try to communicate with each other as best they could, with smiles and hugs and handshakes and trades of Olympic pins and other souvenirs.

Many of the foreign teams wore native costumes when they weren't wearing warm-up uniforms, and that was dazzling too. It was as if I could see the whole world from my balcony, but it was, of course, in an artificial setting where nothing seemed wrong.

On Sunday, July 18, the opening ceremonies packed the Olympic Stadium. It was a whole new thing for me, despite its being my third time around. The first time is a distant memory of a twenty-year-old. The second has been erased by bad memories. But this time, I was consciously drinking it all in. The crowd was huge, the stadium awesome. The show was unique. I grabbed at it and appreciated it as I hadn't done in my two previous Olympics.

That afternoon we had a share-and-prayer meeting in the Village and I wound up giving a little sermonette on self-denial, based on Mark 8:34, the verse about gaining the whole world but losing your own soul. I was talking as if all ten or twelve of us were Christians when it hit me that I didn't know everyone in the room.

"We've been talking like sisters and brothers in the Lord," I said, "and I forgot that there might be somebody here who wants to join the family. Is there anyone who wants to accept Christ?"

Sheila Ingraham nodded. She received Christ that day.

Another thing we talked about at that first meeting was the contrast between the beautiful opening ceremonies we had just attended and the reception we would receive in heaven. We wouldn't be passing by and hailing the queen, we would be praising the King of kings and Lord of lords. It was a precious thought that we'd reunite one day.

Nadia Comaneci was doing her gymnastics thing on television every night, and our roomful of girls would watch it together. We were becoming close. I'd say I was lucky to get in with the girls I did. I was one of only three in the room who had been married, and I was the oldest. It gave me the feeling that they all looked up to me and were rooting for me.

My first heat was on the 23rd, and I was as nervous as anyone else. The Russian, Strykina, was in my heat, and she was the early favorite. Silai, the Rumanian who had finished second behind me at Mexico City, was back for her third Olympics and was in that first heat as well. I wasn't really worried about qualifying for the semis, but the first-day jitters get to everyone in the Olympics.

I was somewhat chagrined by the success Mike Johnson seemed to be having by following the Spirit's leading and distributing literature to the foreign athletes. I thought I had better try it, so I gave a Russian Bible to Strykina. It was an act on my own, motivated only by ,the fact that I thought I wasn't doing as much as Mike. He was following the Spirit's leading and having success. I was doing my own thing, and I fell flat. She glanced at it quickly and

172

left it on the bench beside her. "Thanks for the lesson, Lord," I prayed.

Later, while warming up, I gave a Bible to the Rumanian girl out of a sense of love and concern. She accepted it with appreciation and joy. A few minutes later her coach came over and asked if I would sign it. When she discovered that Alex spoke Hungarian, she talked with him, and he told her how I had come out of retirement to run for Jesus. Ol' Alex was witnessing without even knowing it, ministering in spite of himself!

I overcame the butterflies and qualified easily with a run in the low twos before 70,000 fans. I headed back to the room for a light supper and an early bedtime. Just two more races and I could be the Olympic champion. I felt good and strong and confident. The semifinal was the next day, and the final was the day after that. The thought never entered my head that I wouldn't make it to the final. Confidence was the least of my problems.

In fact, I had no problems. Yet.

Chapter Nineteen

The FINAL SEMI

My day before the semifinal on Saturday was casual.
There was encouragement from all my friends, and Alex
assured me that I looked good and should be in top form.
We were both still hoping that I could run in the low 1:50s
in the final when the chips were down. But first there was
that semi. There would be no final without it.

Most of the day I tried not to think about it. I already
knew my strategy. It was the same as always when you're
just trying to qualify. You go out with the leaders, maintain contact, move when you have to, and assure yourself a spot among the top four. No blasting away unless
it's necessary. Save something for the run for the gold the
next day.

The only thing I feared was that it might take near a
two flat to even qualify with all the quality runners in my
semi. I wanted to be sure to have enough left for the final,
but I would just do what I had to. If I didn't qualify, the
only thing I had to look forward to was the relay. I didn't
want a repeat of Munich.

I wasn't as nervous as I had been before the first heats.
The last thing I remember upon entering the stadium was

that I couldn't be more prepared, mentally, physically, and spiritually.

Since they were scheduled for night, the semis in the women's 800 would be televised back to the United States. I had received letters and calls of encouragement so I knew Christians all over the country, even many who had only heard about me, would be praying as I ran, hoping I would go on to win the gold so I could really share my faith from a platform of honor and notoriety again.

I watched the first semifinal where the German, Anita Weiss, was running. I knew she would be among my stiffest competition in the final. I should have been cheering for Wendy Knudsen and not thinking about the next race and strategy and the German at all. Wendy had run the best race of her life the day before with a 1:59.9, just a tenth of a second off my American record and only the second American woman to break two minutes. In this race, however, she ran a fine 2:01 to finish eighth and last. That tells you what I had to look forward to in the final.

I watched the German girl and tried to judge her tactics. I dreamed about the next day and thought of myself on the starting line with her, thinking about staying with her. She both started fast and finished fast, so there would be little cat and mouse going on. I would just have to hang with her, maybe try to run that first 400 meters in 55 seconds and then call on all my reserves and determination and all I had worked and sweated and sacrificed and prayed for.

But as I stood there watching that first semi and taking myself through the next day's final, my body was tensing up and my muscles were reacting to my thought process. Thinking ahead to the next race before the immediate one has been run is a cardinal sin for a runner. I had never done it before in ten years of international competition, and it was the dumbest thing I could have done.

I stood on the line, waiting for the gun in my own semi, with the thought still running through my mind, *Everyone else is going to be running about a 54 for the first lap. Yup, a smooth 55 will keep you in it and you can go for broke when everyone else does and may the best lady win.* I thought I had a solid chance for a medal, maybe even the gold. Let the German run a 1:53; it would just push me to a 1:52.

The gun sounded, but this wasn't the finals. It was the semis. This isn't the place to run that 55. This is where you run to qualify. But the other girls were leaving me. We were just a few yards down the track and I didn't feel my usual freedom of motion. I increased my speed and reached out more. I still felt awkward. Only 100 meters into the race and I was losing ground. I was struggling, very unusual for this early in the race. It hadn't hit me yet that I had to rectify the situation immediately with this kind of competition.

The other girls were several yards ahead already. I was falling back, losing contact so soon? They were together, of course—no separating yet. I struggled more, realizing that I was already beginning to ache. *No, it's too early. You don't hurt this early. Not until the second lap, not even until the backstretch.* Crazy thoughts raced through my head. *I'm embarrassed. I'm ashamed. What is happening? Let's get it together here.*

Coming out of the first curve and onto the back straight of the first lap I thought if I could only relax and begin to move smoothly, I could move up. I tried, but it just hurt more. I was tense, struggling, frustrated. I tried slowing down into a loping stride, then speeding up. But that did nothing. I forgot to look at the clock as I finished the first lap. If I had only looked, it was right there on the track. I had struggled to 58-second first 400 meters. That's not really that bad, though I was dead last and going nowhere. I could have told myself that I could at least try to duplicate the first lap. Another 58 would have given me a 1:56, better than I had ever run before.

But instead I continued to struggle.

Suddenly I was on the backstretch of the second lap and the other seven girls were already starting to separate as they flew into the far turn. It brought on my first wave of panic. *If I don't move at the 300-meter mark, then I won't be in it.* I still hadn't given up. I had come back before, maybe never from this far back, but why not? It was the Olympics. I'd kill myself if I had to, but I had to qualify.

I shifted gears and tried to lift my legs and arms higher, but my body had tightened up and gone into oxygen debt. It just shut down. I labored just to keep moving and prayed, "God, just let me finish. Don't let me stop here on the track before the whole world." The other girls were into their finishing kicks now, pulling away from me so fast I couldn't even relate to it. I was in my own world of torment, my own race. I had run two races this night. First the finals in my mind, and now this semifinal. And I would pay for it.

As I came around the last curve and onto the straight, the first seven girls were finishing in a bunch, fighting for qualifying positions. I hadn't been able to pick up my pace at all and was really dragging. "Lord, just get me to the end." I finished and bent over, putting my hands on my knees and sucking for air. An official ran over to see if I was all right, and many people assumed I was sick.

But I was all right. I was tight and sore, but I wasn't really hurt. I was disgusted, humiliated, and I had no idea why I had been out of that race from the first step. I had run a 2:07, which I could do backwards right now. It was the worst race I had ever run in my life and I was just flat stunned.

Doris Brown Heritage, the U.S. women's athlete liaison, called down from the stands to see if there was anything she could do, but I was half in shock with a leave-me-

alone attitude. I just waved her off. I plodded into the
locker room and started pulling my sweats out of a wire
basket. Sitting on a cold wooden bench with my head down,
I hardly had the energy to pull on my things.

Wendy Knudsen, who had finished eighth in her semi
too, but with a fine 2:01, came and sat next to me. I
didn't look up. We sat in silence for a few moments.
Then she said, "Madeline, I don't know what to say to
you." She was crying. I wasn't. "I have no words. I don't
know what to say." She put her arms around me and held
me gently for several seconds. "All I can say is that I
really love you—that's all I can say. I just want you to
know that." It was hard for her to talk, but she was so
sweet.

I smiled. "I love you too, Wendy, and I really appreciate that." I stood and left her sitting, shoulders droop-
ing, arms at her sides, crying softly.

I walked out into the tunnel with my bag. A reporter
called after me, "Madeline, we'd like to talk to you."

"Just leave me alone."

By now, Doris had come down from the stands. "Are
you all right?"

I ignored her and kept walking, reporters following
me at a distance. Ironically, they were the only people I
led all day.

Doris caught me and walked beside me, saying nothing. Alex appeared and walked on the other side of me,
and it began to swell in me. I came out of shock into a
full realization that I had blown it, bummed out, failed.
My Olympic hopes were gone. I broke down, and Doris
and Alex engulfed me with their arms.

"That's all right, you just go ahead and cry," Alex said,
fighting his own tears. "It'll be all over in a little while."

I said, "It was horrible!"

Doris touched my face. "Just remember one thing," she
said softly but with authority, "Jesus never fails. He never

fails."

"I know. It just seems like I failed him."

The three of us kept walking around in the tunnel and finally I could talk about it. "You looked fine when you went out on the track," Alex said.

"I was all right," I said. "I wasn't upset. I was loose. I felt like I could run a 1:57 and it wouldn't even hurt." Then I told him I was afraid maybe I had looked ahead to the next race and had taken myself out of the semi that way. He didn't respond, probably because it didn't make any more sense to him than it did to me. And Alex likes things to add up. An international track star, a former world record holder and gold medal winner doesn't look ahead. So, why had I? That's a question I may never be able to answer. But it's the only thing I can think of that caused the worst race of my career.

Alex had told the reporters to wait, so they had kept their distance. Now he wanted to know if I was up to talking with them. Self was saying, "No, don't talk to them. What if you break down in front of them—that's just what they want!"

But the Lord was testing me. "Are you just winning for Jesus, or can you lose for Jesus too? Will you be the big-shot witness while you're on top of the world but not when you have failed?" I knew I had to talk with them. It was painful, but I realized the gold I had been running for was the gold of reaching souls, even in the midst of depression.

I turned to Doris. "Well, in all things, give thanks," I said.

"That's true, Mad."

In my mind, I finished the verse, ". . . for this is the will of God concerning you."

"That's beautiful," Alex said, and he let the reporters have at me.

They flooded me with the expected questions, and I

tried to explain what had happened as logically as I could. One broke in, "But you're experienced. This is your third Olympics. You should know better than to look ahead."

"I know, but I guess I'm human." I told them that I believed the Bible when it says in Romans 8:28 that all things work together for good to those who love God and are called according to his purpose. "Even though I'm hurting inside, yet I feel that the victory is mine."

"But you're out of the finals. How will the victory be yours?"

"There are other victories than on that track," I said. "And I still have a promise to fulfill. I will give of my best to God, and I won't quit until I do. That means the race in Maryland against the Russians after the Olympics."

Fatigue and disappointment sought to defeat me, and I felt the Lord was really putting me through something, but I returned to the stands to watch the men's finals in the 100-meter dash, probably among the most difficult things I have ever done. Many of my friends were there, and a lot of the spectators recognized me. I felt like the world's largest object lesson in failure, but I went and sat with Alex anyway. The Lord was about to give me strength to face a myriad of trials, even before I had the chance to adequately mourn my own loss.

Chapter Twenty

WHERE IS GOD NOW?

As Alex and I found our seats to watch the finals of the men's 100-meter dash, I could feel a hundred eyes looking right through my body. I sensed the love and sympathy of my friends. The love I needed. The sympathy I could do without. There was no feeling sorry for myself. I was crushed, but I had no one to blame but myself.

People treated me as if I'd had a death in the family: me. The Lord was giving me strength to smile and say, "Hey, that's just the way things go sometimes, you know."

I was really pulling for Harvey Glance, our young hopeful in the men's 100. He was always ready with a funny line, constantly keeping us laughing, and yet really a gentleman. We had encouraged each other during the heats and semis, and I'd grown to really like him.

The 100 is probably the most pressure-packed race in all of track, especially, at the international level—a glamor event. The stadium was full but you could have heard a pin drop when the men took their marks. After the gun, pandemonium erupts and for just ten seconds, a runner must do everything right. One missed step, one hesitation, one slip, one hitch, and he can forget it. Think of it, these guys who run the 100 meters in 10 seconds are averaging 10 meters per second! The start has to be perfect, runners bursting away from the blocks with the sound of the gun, digging in, staying low, raising the arms, and pumping furiously. And all the while the body must be smooth, with an economy of motion.

As the sprinters gradually lift into upright running position, the good starters have already established leads. The middle of the run goes to the man with the fastest legs, while the last 20 meters or so belongs to the man with strength and endurance who can lift higher, push harder, maintain his form better. Then it's a precise lean at the end to edge out the competitors by literally hundredths of a second. Often the eight finalists will finish within two-tenths of a second of each other, and the first four within a few hundredths.

Hasely Crawford was the man for this night, running a perfect hundred for the gold. Harvey ran well and his time was good. He was an eyelash behind the winner, it seemed, but three runners had beaten him. Later, outside the stadium, he was really dejected. He had wanted a medal, and not just any medal. He wanted the gold.

"You ran a really good race," I told him.

"No, mistakes, mistakes," he said bitterly.

"You wanna tell me about it?"

"Well, I was concentrating on the start so much, knowing I would need it to get the jump on Borzov [Valery, of the U.S.S.R.] and Quarrie [Don, of Jamaica], that I forgot all about the finish. I didn't drive in strong. If I had just driven in harder, the medal would be mine." He was near tears and unaware that I had lost my race too.

"Hey, Harvey, I know what it feels like to make mistakes, man, but you have to go on. You can't just stop right here and let it get to you so bad. It's going to hurt, sure, but it's over now. There's nothing more you can do about it just running it over and over in your mind. You have a relay to run yet, and you need to be ready for it. Analyze your 100, learn from it, and then leave it alone."

I was listening as I spoke, because it was not really me talking. In myself I didn't have the strength to be giving a young man counsel that I myself needed so badly.

Anxious to get back to my room and just have a good cry, I headed out but ran into Evie Dennis, the women's manager. "Madeline, Chaundra Cheeseborough's pulled a muscle."

I couldn't believe it. What else could go wrong? Chaundra was to run in the 100, the 200, and a relay. "Where is she?" Evie pointed me to a training room, but before I got there I saw Rick Wolhuter, the U.S. 800-meter runner who had just been disqualified in his heat. He hadn't heard about the charge and was of course shocked when I told him. He looked hurt and puzzled, uncertain what to do.

"Look, Rick," I said, "don't get too excited, because they might review it and put you in again. Dr. Walker (the head coach) is in now making a verbal complaint." I didn't know what the chances were, but I had to give Rick something to hope for. (The complaint was upheld, Rick's disqualification was reversed, and he went on to run in the finals.)

It seemed that God knew I was not yet ready to handle my own emotions, so he kept throwing other people's troubles in my way. It was a challenge, as if he were saying, "You would have dealt with these people in love and generosity last week. Deal with them now." My faith was being tested to the hilt. Could I be a Christian, a shining light, from a valley as well as from a hilltop?

When I got into the training room, we saw that it was not Chaundra Cheeseborough but Brenda Moorhead, our top sprinter, who had pulled a muscle. She lay still, almost in shock. It hurt me terribly to see her that way. "Oh, God," I prayed.

I went to her. "What happened?"

I was just running—" she said, but she couldn't go on. I asked the trainer how bad it was, and he tried to make it sound like just a strain. But we all knew. I said that I thought she had run smoothly in the 100, so it couldn't be too bad, but I didn't say that I had noticed that there was not the patented Moorhead third acceleration. That's right, in the 100-meter dash she actually accelerates out of the blocks, again as she hits her stride, and then again with 10 meters to go. No one else anywhere has ever run like that. But that third acceleration was gone at Montreal.

It made me so sick to see such a beautiful girl and fantastic sprinter lying there that I knew if I so much as opened my mouth I would scream. I paced the room, ready to burst, and the only ones who tried to console mouthed meaningless platitudes. I knew all along that the only Person who could make any sense of this was the Lord.

An ambulance arrived to take Brenda to a clinic, and I decided to stay with her. She was very lonely and frightened. As they wheeled her into the ambulance and stalled around waiting for the official clearance, gawkers in the tunnel stared and speculated among themselves as to who it was and what had happened. "Don't let them bother you," I told her. "If you were out there, you'd be asking who was in the ambulance too."

When we got to the clinic it was more of the same. Waiting, signing, clearing. Brenda didn't look good. "How you doin', Bren'?" I asked. She nodded without smiling. Someone had told her to be brave and not to cry. I disagreed.

"Hey," I said, "if you feel like crying, go right ahead. You'll probably feel better. I don't know what's gonna come of all this, but don't be afraid to cry." I handed her a jacket, using the excuse "in case you're cold," but she knew what it was for. She draped it over her head and just sobbed in its privacy. My heart broke for her.

But I didn't have a jacket to hang over my head.

After Brenda was treated and her leg iced, we took her

back to her room at the Village. Harvey Glance stopped in to see her, and by now she could talk. They chatted while I watched television, the ache building inside me. Thankfully, they didn't rerun my event on the screen. I don't think I could have taken it.

But while I was idly watching the other events, my race ran through my mind and I could feel it swelling. I pressed my lips tight together and shook my head slowly. Tears burned my eyes, and I fought them with all that was in me. I wanted to rush out to the terrace and just let it all out, but I couldn't. Not with the kids there. I had to be strong and I knew it. I just couldn't break down in front of them. But God wasn't through testing me. A split second after I had won the battle over my emotions, Harvey turned to me.

"How'd you do in the semis, Mad?" he said.

I looked at him squarely. "Harvey, I'm just sittin' here thinkin' about it. I didn't do."

Brenda sat up. "What? What happened?"

"I ran the worst race of my life and finished last, that's what happened," I said, matter-of-factly.

"Mad, I can't see how you could have been with me all this time if that happened to you," Brenda said.

"For real?" Harvey said. "And then you were down there talking to me after the 100. I didn't even know."

"Yeah," I said, "but you have to be thankful in all things, and it wouldn't do me any good to go running away from everyone else's troubles just because I've got a few of my own. That doesn't mean I'm thankful about what happened, but I can still thank Jesus that he's on the throne in spite of it."

I finally got back to my room and was able to reflect a bit. In the flesh I was tempted to question God, to demand to know why he would let me come out of retirement and work so hard and sacrifice so much, just to be humiliated and lose out there before the whole world. But the battle raged. I determined to find his perfect will in what had happened. It was not easy. I argued with myself for hours.

I knew that God had pushed me into consoling Harvey and then Rick Wolhuter and then Brenda so I could listen to myself. There was, frankly, no one else on the team with my spiritual reserves, so neither was there anyone who could console me any better than I could. Indirectly, he was having me console myself.

Of course, he had sent Doris and Wendy right after the race, and I'll never forget Wendy telling me so sincerely that all she had to say was that she loved me. It was as if the Lord himself had visited me and said, "Hey, what you will go through now will be rough, but I still love you. And I will use you."

There had been a lot of people who had jumped on my bandwagon and had opted for my type of Christianity because "it was obviously working" for me. In other words, they translated it into athletic success, talent, fame. God had promised he would use me to shine at the Olympics, but, as I said before, he never promised it would be from the mountaintop, where less light is needed anyway.

Where was God now? Where were all those people who could really get into what I was into, as long as it meant winning? Even some Christians were caught up in that. They figured that if I dedicated my running career to God, he was obliged to honor it with success. I had won so many meets, so many races, broken so many records. Now what? Could I be a loser for Jesus?

People came into the room at different times as the clock approached midnight. They looked at me and then looked away quickly. It irritated me, but, of course, they couldn't have done anything right: I didn't want to be ignored. I didn't want to be consoled. And I probably wouldn't have liked it if people had tried to be loose and light and pretended nothing had happened. I didn't win, and they couldn't either.

It began to dawn on me that God had been preparing me for this. I'd had the feeling ever since I came out of retirement that it wasn't supposed to be so easy. I had been given a mission which included a cross to bear. I hadn't really borne it until now. I had read books of people who got to crucial stages in their careers and failed. I had been led to read of the kings of the Old Testament until I was sick and tired of kings who were always losing battles and being killed.

The Lord had been warning me, but I just followed him, not seeing far ahead. I trusted him, and if I missed his cues, that made it a little harder to take. But I would still trust.

Karen Smith, a javelin-thrower, came in and joined the silent crowd in the room. She broke the ice. She patted me and said, "Well, you're still a champion in my eyes." Immediately, everyone in the room picked up on it and repeated it in their own way. "Yeah, you're still a champ." "You're my champ, Mad." I smiled.

When an old friend called, it was like a gift from heaven. "You're sitting there in that room, and everyone is acting funny about you, right?" he said.

"You got it," I said.

"Why don't you go out with me and my friends and just get away for a few hours?"

I couldn't think of anything I'd rather have done right then. In the car, on the way to hear a music group, Larry (not his real name) put on an Andraé Crouch tape. I was telling Larry and his friends that I knew Andraé and that he wrote the song for my album and all, and then a song came on that just was meant specifically for me that very night. It was the reason God had led Larry to call me, I'm convinced.

I began to sing along, crying and laughing at the same time. "Even when the cold winds blow, dear Lord, I want You to know—I'll still love You, Lord, Oh, I'll still love You.

. . . Even if I never reach fame and people don't remember my name, I'll still love you. . . . Nothing shall separate me from Your love, no, no, no!" * I went on, singing from my heart, "Uh, uh, I don't care, I'm gonna love you anyway!"

I told Larry, "If nothing else happens tonight, I needed to hear that song. That spoke the sentiments of my heart. I didn't realize the depth of my own love for Christ. I love Jesus beyond all things. I feel like I've lost everything but him, and because of him I can keep my sanity."

He was glad to hear me talk like that, and then I was ready to talk about my race, to really get it out of my system. When he took me back to the Village at 2:30 that morning, he gave me a quick pep talk about getting my thing together for the 1600-meter relay.

Still, though, I couldn't sleep. I knew I loved Jesus more than ever, but the battle continued. I couldn't get my mind off the race and the "if only's." I would much rather have been losing sleep worrying about how I was going to do in the finals. But here I was, after everything, having to deal with defeat. I prayed long and hard, and the Lord began to answer about an hour or so later when I had about come to the end of myself. I was exhausted, but I couldn't sleep. I was trusting God for his will, but still I wanted to know what it was.

That's the great thing about a real communication with God. If you're in the Word and praying every day, you don't have to settle for platitudes like "Well, maybe this is the Lord's will. I'll just blindly trust him." He will impress upon you deeper truths, things to make you understand more clearly.

I'm not saying I was looking for the reason that I ran poorly: I had already figured that out to my satisfaction. I pulled the move of a novice and tied myself up by

---

* "I'll Still Love You." Words and music by Andraé Crouch. © Copyright 1975 by Lexicon Music, Inc. Used by permission.

thinking too far ahead. The question was, why right then?
Why here? Why me, hardly a novice?

In the wee hours of the morning the Lord spoke to my
heart and reminded me again that a light that shines from
a mountaintop can be consumed by the other light around
it. It doesn't mean a lot, it blends in. But if the light shines
from the depths of a valley, it penetrates and consumes
the darkness. I thanked the Lord for that word, and then
he caused me to parallel my experience with that of Jesus.

On the way to the cross the people who had been with
him, following him, praising him, identifying with him,
were long gone. As long as he had been speaking as they
had never heard one speak before, or as long as he was
healing the sick or making the blind see, or feeding the
multitudes, everybody was for him. But when he was
beaten and whipped and spit upon and cursed and hanged
naked, where were they? He was still God. But he was
alone.

The Lord reminded me of my humiliation and shame
and defeat and promised that as I had taken part in a
small way in his suffering and death, so would I take part
in his resurrection and reign. It was just the beginning!
Now that I had died, I could live and reign with Christ! I
knew more succinctly what he was all about.

The Lord was ready to do really magnificent things,
and I was going to be part of it. Joy surged through me
with the realization, and I praised the Lord for comfort-
ing me. My race would still come back to me and haunt
me at times. (In fact, it still does.) But regardless of the
specific reason for it, I knew it was necessary. Then the
Lord gave me Galatians 5:7 and I wept in relief.

A few of us had decided to meet for another prayer-and-
share time that Sunday morning. I wasn't ready for the
Lord to begin using me right away, but his timing has

always been different from mine. It was a simple little gathering I would never forget.

We met in a small room in the International Building. The word had spread quickly, so there were about twenty of us, plus newsmen and some cameramen.

I went in with a prayer on my lips. "Lord, minister to me. I really want to hear from you."

When we finally settled into a circle, Carol, who worked in the Pastoral Room (a religious gathering place) at the Village, began to speak.

She said the Lord had given her something the night before from Exodus about Moses at the burning bush. He had asked God, "Who am I that you should send me?"

"When I think of the world-class athletes I ran into here, and maybe when you athletes think of the foreign athletes you try to share with," Carol went on, "maybe you ask yourself the same question. Maybe you're feeling inadequate. Here's a person from a different country, a different culture, a different thought process even, and who is little ol' you to be telling him about Jesus?"

Then she moved on and had us looking up some verses, including some in Ephesians about partaking in Christ's death. "I don't know how many of you here have already competed," she said. "And maybe you didn't do what you wanted to do. Maybe you were looking for the gold, but you lost and you feel like you haven't done anything. Maybe you were humiliated.

"Maybe you didn't swim like you thought you should have, or maybe you didn't run as fast as you could. And now you feel like you've failed the Lord. You were going for the gold and now there's no chance. But remember Romans 8:28, 'All things work together for good to those who love God. . . .'"

By now, tears were flooding silently down my face. When she stopped talking there was complete silence. The Lord was speaking to me.

I broke the silence. "I've got something I want to share," I said shakily. "Carol, I thank God for you, for just being open to the Holy Spirit. You don't realize that what you have just said was a message directed to me from the Holy Spirit." She looked puzzled. "I just ran one of the worst races of my life, and it hurts." I couldn't say any more for a while. Everyone was crying.

"If you could just bear with me, this is something the Lord wants me to share for my own breakthrough." I told how the Lord had dealt with me after my loss, and how he continued to minister to me into the early hours of the morning. He didn't want me to say I was just praising him in spite of it all. He wanted me to admit that I was nothing, that it was crushing me, I couldn't handle it. But he had handled it through me. He had given me strength to the point where from a beginning that was shaky I moved to a finish of exaltation and encouragement.

"The battle is there for us to fight, but the victory is already won."

After swimmer John Naber, tracksters Fred Newhouse, Tommy Haines, and Doris Brown Heritage gave their testimonies, we had communion, sang "Let Us Break Bread Together," and closed in sentence prayer.

I called Wanda in Cleveland and told her, "I feel like I've been crucified, but I'm rising from the grave with the power of Jesus Christ and now I'm an eagle who will stir the nest." Day after day, even through the end of the Olympics, I was able to deal with more individual athletes who suffered painful defeats and disappointments.

Always I was able to reach into my own reservoir and identify with them. I told them that if I could make it, they could too. It opened doors to share about Jesus. People came to Christ because I died on that track.

EPILOGUE

Madeline Manning Jackson was replaced by Sheila Ingra-
ham in the 1600-meter relay in Montreal and ran just one
more 800 before retiring. Her 1:57.9 against the Russians
in Maryland broke her own American record by nearly
two full seconds. She finished third.

Not long after returning to her home in Cleveland, she
resigned her position at the Salvation Army Hough Multi-Purpose Center to devote full time to her speaking and
singing ministry. Her album, *Running for Jesus,* pro-
duced by Paragon, released under the Newpax label, and
distributed by Word, was released in October 1976 and is
available at Christian bookstores.

You may write her at 13855 Superior Road, Apt. 2005,
East Cleveland, Ohio 44118.